Gillian Wearing

MASS OBSERVATION

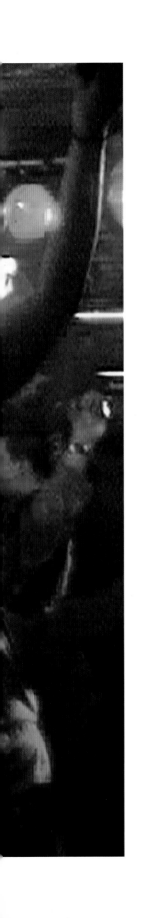

Gillian Wearing

MASS OBSERVATION

Exhibition curator
Dominic Molon

Essays by
Dominic Molon
Barry Schwabsky

Museum of
Contemporary Art,
Chicago

MERRELL

770.92 WEA (handwritten)

First published 2002 by
Museum of Contemporary Art, Chicago
220 East Chicago Avenue
Chicago, Illinois 60611-2604
and

Merrell Publishers Limited
42 Southwark Street
London SE1 1UN
www.merrellpublishers.com

This publication accompanies the exhibition
Gillian Wearing: Mass Observation organized by
the Museum of Contemporary Art, Chicago.

Exhibition venues

Museum of Contemporary Art, Chicago
October 19, 2002 – January 19, 2003

Institute of Contemporary Art, Philadelphia
September 3 – December 14, 2003

This exhibition is generously supported by Margot
and George Greig, Robert and Sylvie Fitzpatrick,
The Elizabeth Firestone Graham Foundation, and
The British Council.

The Museum of Contemporary Art (MCA) is a
nonprofit, tax-exempt organization. The MCA's
exhibitions, programming and operations are
member-supported and privately funded through
contributions from individuals, corporations,
and foundations. Additional support is provided
through the Illinois Arts Council, a state agency;
and CityArts Program 4 Grant from the City of
Chicago Department of Cultural Affairs. Additional
significant support is provided by the State of
Illinois. Air transportation services are provided by
American Airlines, the official airline of the
Museum of Contemporary Art.

Produced by the Publications Department of the
Museum of Contemporary Art, Chicago: Hal Kugeler,
Director; Kari Dahlgren, Associate Director;
Kythzia Jurado, Designer; and Tony Neuhoff, Editor.

Edited by Kari Dahlgren and Tony Neuhoff
Designed by Kythzia Jurado

Distributed in the USA by Rizzoli International
Publications, Inc., through St. Martin's Press,
175 Fifth Avenue, New York, New York 10010

A catalog record for this book is available from the
Library of Congress.

British Library Cataloguing-in-Publication Data:
Molon, Dominic
Gillian Wearing : mass observation
1.Wearing, Gillian, 1963 Criticism and interpretation
I.Title II.Schwabsky, Barry III.Wearing, Gillian, 1963
IV.Museum of Contemporary Art (Chicago, Ill.)
709.2

ISBN 1 85894 178 4

Printed and bound in Italy

JACKET AND PAGES 2–3,
99–107, AND 116
BROAD STREET
2001
Six-screen color video
projection with sound
40 minutes
Edition of 2 aside
from 2 artist's proofs

Unless indicated in the captions, all works by
Gillian Wearing are courtesy of Maureen Paley
Interim Art, London.

CONTENTS

FOREWORD

Gillian Wearing's work demonstrates an astonishingly complex understanding of the alternately comic and tragic experience of everyday life. Emerging in the early 1990s at a critical moment for British art, Wearing has distinguished herself as one of the most important artists of her generation. Her video and photography, much of which documents the psychological traumas and tics of ordinary people, presents an extraordinarily profound new visualization of human behavior. The Museum of Contemporary Art is proud to be the first American institution to present a solo exhibition devoted to Wearing's visionary work.

This exhibition has been made possible by the generous support of Margot and George Greig, The Elizabeth Firestone Graham Foundation, and The British Council. We also wish to thank American Airlines for their continued support.

The lenders to the exhibition receive our warmest gratitude for sharing their works with a larger audience. We also thank Claudia Gould, Director of the Institute of Contemporary Art, Philadelphia, for her early interest in bringing the exhibition to the East Coast and for her consistent support.

And finally, to Gillian Wearing we extend our deepest thanks and appreciation for her incredible exhibition, her generous spirit, and her captivating reflections of the world around us.

ROBERT FITZPATRICK
Pritzker Director
Museum of Contemporary Art
Chicago

ACKNOWLEDGMENTS

Many people have worked tirelessly on this project and to all of them I extend my heartfelt thanks. I am especially grateful for those who pledged their support to the exhibition, including Margot and George Greig, Robert and Sylvie Fitzpatrick, The Elizabeth Firestone Graham Foundation, and The British Council. I also extend my sincere thanks to the following lenders: the Musée d'Art Moderne de la Ville de Paris; Eileen and Peter Norton; Anthony T. Podesta; and the Goetz Collection, Munich.

At the MCA, Pritzker Director Robert Fitzpatrick ardently supported the exhibition from beginning to end. James W. Alsdorf Chief Curator Elizabeth Smith, Manilow Senior Curator Francesco Bonami, and Associate Curator Staci Boris were also extraordinarily encouraging. The exhibition was installed with enormous care by Scott Short and his crew and by Dennis O'Shea. Meridith Gray expertly coordinated the shipping, and Lela Hersh handled the tour of the exhibition. Patrick McCukser, with Julie Havel and Sarah Kirby, secured funding for the exhibition.

I wish to thank the Publications Department, led by Hal Kugeler, for producing this catalogue. Kari Dahlgren and Tony Neuhoff thoughtfully edited the text, with assistance from Trisha Beck, and Kythzia Jurado provided the wonderful design. Hugh Merrell and Matt Hervey from our copublisher Merrell Publishers Limited were enthusiastic collaborators. Barry Schwabsky's essay provides a singularly rich and complex understanding of Gillian's work.

Claudia Gould, Director of the Institute of Contemporary Art in Philadelphia, showed immediate interest in the exhibition and I wish to thank her and her staff for their presentation of it.

Special thanks also go to Tim Blum, Achim Borchardt-Hume, Amy Corle, Lisa Corrin, Russell Ferguson, Michael Gaughan, Suzanne Geiss, and Michael Landy.

It's hard to imagine how this project might have been done without Maureen Paley and James Lavender at Maureen Paley Interim Art, London. They were wonderful to work with. Jay Gorney and Carole Wagemans from Gorney Bravin + Lee, New York, were also terrific in providing additional support. Tom Cullen assisted with the technological aspects of the project and was a total pleasure to work with.

Finally, I extend my warmest thanks to Gillian Wearing, for her inspired work, for making the entire experience a pleasure, and for a wonderful night out in Birmingham!

DOMINIC MOLON
Associate Curator
Museum of Contemporary Art
Chicago

Dominic Molon

I mean if you scrutinize reality closely enough, if in some way you really, really get
to it, it becomes fantastic. . . . It really is totally fantastic that we look like this and you
sometimes see that very clearly in a photograph. Something is ironic in the world
and it has to do with the fact that what you intend never comes out like you intend it.
What I'm trying to describe is that it's impossible to get out of your skin and into
somebody else's. And that's what all this is a little bit about. That somebody else's
tragedy is not the same as your own.

— Diane Arbus

OBSERVING THE MASSES

SIXTY MINUTE SILENCE
(detail), 1996
Color video projection with sound
60 minutes
Artist's proof
Collection of Anthony T.
Podesta, Podesta Mattoon,
Washington, D.C.

THE POLITICS OF GENDER, SEXUALITY, ETHNICITY, and other aspects of identity
have recently prompted new moral and philosophical considerations about the "other" in
works of art: who is being depicted, by whom, and toward what end. At best, the resulting
paradigm shift has encouraged the presentation of a broader and more diverse range of
cultural perspectives: at worst, it is responsible for both a vogue for the exotic in the guise
of well-intentioned inclusiveness and a rhetoric of exclusion that makes claims about what
subjects can or cannot be represented. One of the most interesting and effective responses
of artists to this particular situation is what Hal Foster has identified as an "ethnographic
turn,"[1] a method of collecting and re-presenting material based on observation of human
society and culture that emulates ethnographic practice. Work produced in this manner
often takes the form of documentary photography or video, sometimes paired with
explanatory text or narrative. This style follows the logic and aesthetics of conceptual art
in which only the most fundamental forms of information are placed on display — for
example, the simple text works of On Kawara or Lawrence Weiner or the straightforward
photographic displays of Ed Ruscha and Bernd and Hilla Becher. While some artists in
the 1980s and 1990s applied this technique as social critique and neo-agitprop, others used
the ethnographic turn to meditate on more universal issues of everyday existence. Aiming
to complicate ethnography's conclusions or hypotheses based on detached observations
made in the field, some artists engaged with their subjects in a more participatory or
interactive fashion. As Norman Bryson observed: "New style ethnography . . . deliberately
revers[es] the 'objective' and 'scientific' stance of the old, bad anthropology. It seeks to
make the observer and observed into equal partners, joint collaborators in the production
of intercultural knowledge."[2]

Gillian Wearing's videos and photographs from the early 1990s to the present engage in this process through the documentation of alternately shocking, amusing, and tragic stories and behavior of ordinary people from Britain. Wearing repeatedly creates situations in which first-hand "evidence" is offered about particularly telling experiences, or in which she translates uncomfortable moments that she has witnessed. Her narrative work draws heavily on mundane occurrences, resulting in cinematic fiction that discomfortingly resembles reality. She emerged at an auspicious moment in contemporary art, one characterized not only by the development of ethnographically inspired work, but also by the overwhelmingly positive critical reception of video installation and photography. While much of this work has focused on visually dissecting cinematic references or globalized society, Wearing's has distinguished itself with its altered-verité treatment of the more ambivalent moral, social, and emotional issues of everyday existence.

Wearing's work resonates with the pre–World War II British social documentary project Mass-Observation. The group, founded by Charles Madge, Tom Harrisson, and Humphrey Jennings in 1937, aimed to "collect a mass of data based upon practical observation, on the everyday lives of all types of people."[3] Eschewing the exoticism of a cultural "other," Mass-Observation turned the scrutinizing lens of ethnographic practice on British culture itself and "anticipated later conceptions of reflexive ethnography and anthropology as cultural criticism."[4] This was perhaps the most radically provocative aspect of their project: "[T]he assumption that a 'civilised' culture like Britain in the 1930s could be approached using the same language of ritual and belief that guided anthropologists in their discussion of 'uncivilised' cultures challenged any assumed 'natural' superiority of western culture."[5] A key aspect of Mass-Observation's method was to provide a then unheard-of agency to their anthropological subjects, encouraging active participation in the research process, and thereby "giving working-class and middle-class people a chance to speak for themselves, about themselves."[6]

Wearing's work similarly features raw, firsthand accounts of everyday people, mostly from London or elsewhere in England. Yet the material that she collects is mitigated by an ironically detached re-presentation that uses masquerade, neutral backgrounds, and vocal mediation — visual and sonic devices that create a sense of distance between artist and subject. This experientially ambiguous interzone also sets up an unsettling dynamic between viewer and subject, one reminiscent of the effect of Diane Arbus's 1960s and 1970s photographs of awkwardly ordinary people and others pushed to the periphery of society. Wearing's projects recall much of the strangeness of Arbus's imagery — and with that, the viewer's complex and emotionally fraught response of curiosity, sympathy, and superiority — yet view dysfunction through the more empathic lens of the contemporary ethnographic approach.

Wearing's photographs and videos from the early 1990s set up an ongoing dialectic between public and private — the secret *vox* of the British *populi* are recast and presented in the public forum of art. *Signs that say what you want them to say and not Signs that say what someone else wants you to say* (1992–93, pp. 26 and 29) is the result of the deceptively simple project of approaching people in the street, asking them to write the first thought

DANCING IN PECKHAM
1994
Color video, silent
25 minutes
Edition of 10 aside from
1 artist's proof

to come to their minds on uniformly sized blank cards, and photographing them holding their statements. This series of photographs is both a cumulative portrait of city life as well as an on-the-spot sampling of a collective urban unconscious. A radically different work created in the public sphere, *Dancing in Peckham* (1994, p. 13) depicts Wearing herself grooving in the center of a shopping mall arcade to a soundtrack (Nirvana's "Smells Like Teen Spirit" and Gloria Gaynor's "I Will Survive") that only she can hear. In this work, Wearing internalized the dance moves of a stranger she had seen in a club. The subsequent performance — a cultural experiment of sorts — is a demonstration of how certain bodily movements appear normal in one context yet utterly bizarre in another. *Homage to the woman with the bandaged face who I saw yesterday down Walworth Road* (1995, pp. 32–33), another examination of human behavior conducted in the urban "field," grew out of Wearing's curiosity about the woman described in the title and her desire to be this woman for a day. Cameras both within and outside the mask record the tragicomic events of Wearing's walk down Walworth Road dressed as the woman with the stark white bandaged face, providing the viewer with an unsettling view through the eyes of a freakish "other." Wearing's deft conceptual gestures in these works emphasize the alternately comical and disturbing results of exposing the private or humbling thoughts, actions, and visions of everyday people.

One of the most visible and complicated social entities is the police force — a group relied upon for its maintenance of law and order yet frequently susceptible to such human failings as the corruption of power. In her video installation *Sixty Minute Silence* (1996, pp. 10 and 43–45) Wearing used a fixed camera and an impossibly long pose to create an awkwardly personal moment. What appears at first glance to be a backlit photographic portrait of a group of British police officers reveals through closer scrutiny almost imperceptible shifts and blinks among the ranks. The presence of police gives many people, including Wearing, feelings of guilt and dread: "I still cannot meet the gaze of a policeman and normally bow my head even though I've never done anything to be arrested for in my life."[7] *Sixty Minute Silence*, despite its display of group solidarity and potential force, strips the officers of their power by holding them raptly before the viewer.

Wearing's reversal of the power relations between viewers and viewed recalls aspects of Michel Foucault's *Discipline and Punish: The Birth of the Prison*, the celebrated study of power and control and its relationship to the human body. Foucault wrote, "The exercise of discipline presupposes a mechanism that coerces by means of observation; an apparatus in which the techniques that make it possible to see induce effects of power and in which, conversely, the means of coercion make those on whom they are applied clearly visible."[8] In effect, Wearing set up "the perfect disciplinary apparatus" in *Sixty Minute Silence*, one that "make[s] it possible for a single gaze to see everything constantly."[9] A sense of group identity in the portrait begins to disintegrate and the ordinary individuality of each particular member begins to assert itself. The police, having become "prisoners" of the viewer's penetrating gaze and kept silent by the dictates of Wearing's concept, one-by-one become "clearly visible" as individual and ultimately "ordinary" human beings.

Sixty Minute Silence echoes two radically different works by contemporaries of Wearing: Sharon Lockhart's epic structuralist film *Teatro Amazonas* and Vanessa Beecroft's performances, such as *VB35*, executed at the Guggenheim Museum, New York, in 1998. The former depicts an audience of citizens from Manaus, Brazil, seated in the ornate, nineteenth-century European opera house of the title, which is incongruously located in the midst of their Amazon-region city. The spectators in the film seem to watch the viewers of the film while both audiences experience a twenty-six minute choral performance that gradually fades to reveal the ambient noise of both groups. Where Lockhart's film mirrors the audiences through architectural space (the Teatro and the theater where the film is being screened), *Sixty Minute Silence* encourages a more fluid and singular viewing as an installation. While the police were kept still for sixty minutes and both audiences of *Teatro Amazonas* sit politely for the duration, the viewers of Wearing's work are at liberty to position and reposition themselves around the work for as long as they choose. Lockhart, in fact, gave her audience free rein of the theater space during the performance, temporarily turning the tables on the symbolic imposition of Western culture and the power it represents. *Sixty Minute Silence*'s captive policemen enjoyed no such freedom and thus stand or sit perpetually in formation to be watched by those they might ordinarily monitor.

Sharon Lockhart
Teatro Amazonas
1999
35 mm color film with sound
Courtesy of Blum & Poe,
Santa Monica, Calif.

Beecroft's performances typically present groups of attractive young women dressed (and more often undressed) in a rigid formation. They stand mute and remote, present in a physical sense but utterly isolated from human contact by the strictly defined limits of Beecroft's composition. Here the experience of viewing a group is similar to that of *Sixty Minute Silence* in that the blank uniformity of the whole dissolves when the particularities of the individuals become apparent. In terms of the exchange of power, Wearing's and Beecroft's works are even more similar. While one is offered

a certain scopophilic appreciation of the revealed female form in Beecroft's performances, this dissipates over time as the initial eroticism of the situation gives way to the weirdly mute presence of the figures and the simultaneously painterly and sculpture-like arrangement of colors and shapes. Likewise, in *Sixty Minute Silence*, whatever thrills one might temporarily enjoy in observing the captive police are tempered by the photographic and sculptural nature of Wearing's portrait and by the tension between the overall stasis of the group and individuals' movements.

A more private social group is the family — a deeply influential source of socialization, discipline, and control. As the psychoanalytic theories of Sigmund Freud (and virtually any "true crime" television program) have revealed, neuroses result from aspects of the parent-child relationship that are repressed yet manifest themselves in the behavioral patterns of the mature adult. The most charged familial relationships — those between the adult and children of opposite sexes — have the greatest effect on the adult that one becomes. Wearing's video *2 into 1* (1997, pp. 47–53) was originally created for a BBC 2 television series called *Expanding Pictures* and is an alarmingly candid deconstruction of the mother-son relationship. In this work, a middle-aged mother, Hilary, and her two sons, Alex and Lawrence, lip-synch to recordings of one another's voices so that they seem to be describing themselves as the other sees them. The results are disturbing: the boys provide blunt criticisms of their mother's appearance, driving, and intellectual capacity, as well as more complimentary observations about her cooking and her compassionate nature — all of which the mother rephrases through her own mouth. This footage is intercut with the boys mouthing to the words of Hilary discussing their temper tantrums and their often cruel behavior toward her, as well as her own frustrations as a mother and even her psychosexual hang-ups. Beyond the fundamentally bizarre age and gender displacement created by the shifted voices, it is unsettling to hear all three parties repeating the innermost thoughts and feelings of each other about themselves. Wearing, through the sheer audacity of asking ordinary people to participate in this soul-baring, psychoanalytic situation and through the use of a clever audiovisual technique, broke up this family into spoken word parts to reveal the grotesque truths that shape any family unit and lay the groundwork for psychological complications in adult life.

In *2 into 1*'s companion piece, *10 – 16* (1997, pp. 18–19 and 55–59), Wearing similarly used the voices of children ages ten to sixteen lip-synched by adults and retransmitted for the camera. Their stories vary from naively charming — a ten-year-old talking about his tree house and the fun he has there — to the terrifyingly pathological — a thirteen-year-old discussing his disgust at his mother's new girlfriend and his desire to kill them both — to the poignantly depressing — a sixteen-year-old expressing feelings of shame and anxiety about his weight and his sexual explorations. Wearing grafted the frustrations, delusions, and neuroses of the children onto the faces of the adults — including two old ladies having a picnic and a dwarf lolling naked in a bath — prompting consideration of how the tribulations of our past wreak havoc on our mature lives. Both *2 into 1* and *10 – 16* betray the influence of British documentary films such as *The Family*, Franc Roddam and Paul Watson's 1974 observation of a typical British family, and *7 Up* (1964), Michael Apted's unique examination of ordinary seven-year-olds that continued every seven years as the subjects lived through adulthood. The use of testimony from ordinary Britons also recalls the previously noted ethnographic studies of Mass-Observation. In this sense, *2 into 1* and *10 – 16* suggest what James Clifford has described as "ethnographic surrealism," especially when he comments that "ethnography cut with surrealism emerges as the theory and practice of juxtaposition." [10] Wearing's uncanny transformation of documentary material reflects Clifford's observation that the surrealists' "attitude, while comparable to the fieldworker who strives to render the unfamiliar comprehensible, tended to work in the reverse sense, making the familiar strange." [11]

One of Wearing's fictional takes on everyday life, the video installation *Sacha and Mum* (1996, pp. 20–21), also uses a manipulation of sound and image to warp one's perception of what begins as a rather pleasant scene between a mother and daughter. Proceeding from the immediate strangeness of the older woman being fully clothed and the younger woman wearing only a bra and panties, the scene quickly devolves into a violent and abusive struggle between the two. The action is presented in black-and-white (lending it a dreamlike quality) and shown both forward and in reverse, so that the movements often appear even more wildly out of control and the voices sound unreal. The presentation of such a brutal scene of domestic abuse — even between two adults — is shocking. In *Sacha and Mum*, Wearing took a commonplace subject in daily life that seems beyond the reach of such bluntly honest representation and distorted it to make banal malevolence all the more grotesque and real.

Wearing's keen ability to convert the familiar into the shockingly unfamiliar continues in the similarly cinematic installation *I Love You* (1999, pp. 79–85). The work begins in an empty suburban street with a lone street light recalling both René Magritte's surrealist

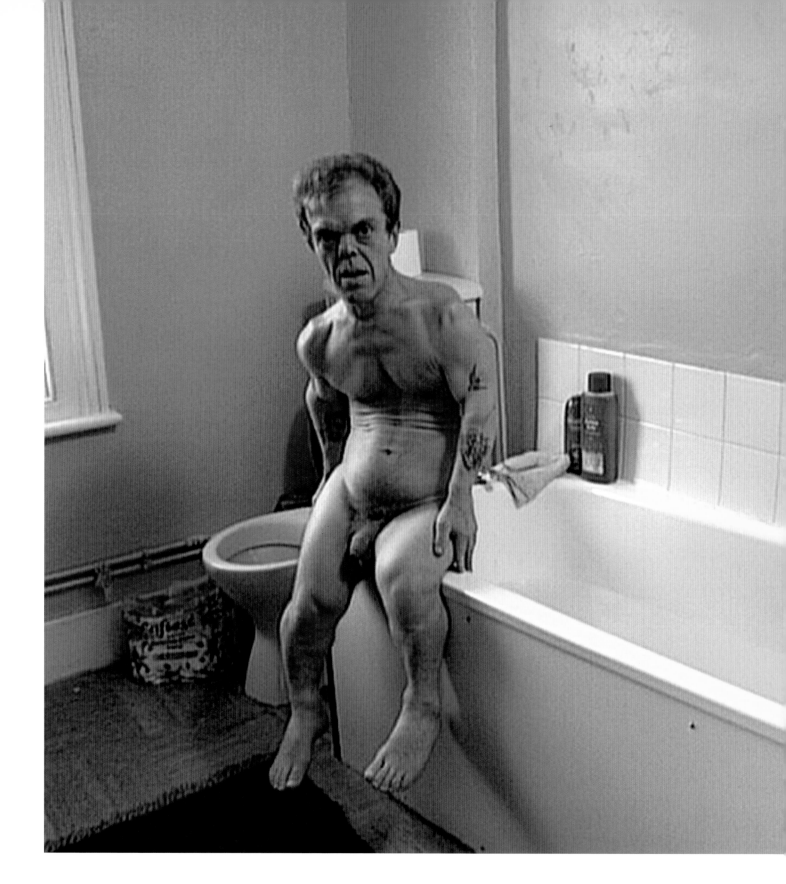

10 – 16
1997
Color video projection
with sound
15 minutes
Edition of 3 aside
from 1 artist's proof

SACHA AND MUM
1996
Black-and-white video
projection with sound
4 minutes
Edition of 3 aside from
1 artist's proof

masterpiece *L'empire des lumières* (*The Dominion of Light*) (1952) and the haunting image of the solitary figure of Father Merrin pausing in front of the O'Neill house before entering to do battle with the devil in the film *The Exorcist* (1973). The four protagonists in *I Love You* pour out of a car that pulls up to the curb, three of them assembling themselves variously around the "star" — a woman who violently staggers back and forth across the lawn and into the house, screaming "I love you" over and over again. This scene is repeated seven times, the tone, inflection, and intent of the woman's delivery of the words changing — sometimes only slightly, sometimes dramatically — each time. Her cries and actions swerve from impassioned pleading to pugilistic anger and anxiety. Foucault's discussion of passion's relationship to insanity corresponds interestingly to the scenes presented in Wearing's video:

> Madness participates both in the necessity of passion and in the anarchy of what, released by this very passion, transcends it and ultimately contests all it implies. Madness ends by being a movement of the nerves and muscles so violent that nothing in the course of images, ideas, or wills seems to correspond to it: this is the case of mania when it is suddenly intensified into convulsions, or when it degenerates into continuous frenzy. [12]

I Love You embodies this irrationality, presenting a woman who has lost both physical and mental control due, apparently, to her intense romantic feelings. The work demonstrates how intense love easily slides into hysteria and manic behavior to completely undermine one's grip on reality.

I Love You is one of Wearing's occasional departures from her typically documentary practice, presenting a dramatized re-creation of an otherwise typical scene. The realism of the scene is complicated by its continual reconstruction, calling to mind films such as Akira Kurosawa's *Rashomon* (1950), in which four different characters provide their recollections of a heinous crime. Whereas that film calls the subjective nature (and therefore the veracity) of "eyewitness testimony" into question, Wearing's film demonstrates the fragility of language by exposing its dependence on phrasing, circumstance, and context. Later in Foucault's discussion about passion and delirium he identifies the role of language in the relationship between the two: "Language is the first and last structure of madness, its constituent form; on language are based all the cycles in which madness articulates its nature. That the

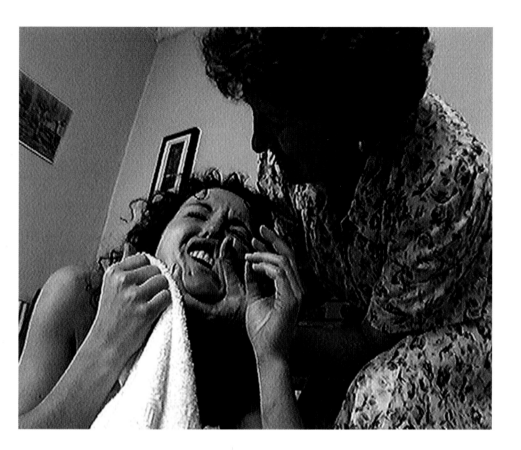

essence of madness can be ultimately defined in the simple structure of a discourse does not reduce it to a purely psychological nature, but gives it a hold over the totality of soul and body."[13] Wearing uses the woman's irrational behavior to demonstrate the instability of language in *I Love You*, reflecting on how the same discourse intended to convey unambiguous sentiments and ideas can also provide the external signs and expressions of psychosis. By structuring the situation in this way, Wearing refrained from presenting a conclusive understanding of passion pushed to the point of delusional obsession, rather creating a work of fiction that reproduces the unsettling ambiguity of real life.

Wearing's videos *Confess all on Video. Don't worry, you will be in disguise. Intrigued? Call Gillian.* (1994, pp. 30–31 and 115) and *Trauma* (2000, pp. 89–93) feature anonymous people wearing masks and, respectively, confessing to things they have done or witnessed and describing events from childhood or adolescence that left them scarred for life. In *Confess all on Video*, the subjects wear all forms of often ridiculous disguise, including a clown's face, bizarre wigs, and a mask of former American president George Bush, making their confessions of criminal activities, voyeurism, and sexual transgressions seem more frightening. Wearing used the masks of adolescent-aged faces in *Trauma*, wanting "the masks to transport [the viewer] back to the defining moment in the wearer's lives. To a time when you wouldn't have been able to see the signs yet on their faces. When the only visible signs might perhaps have been in their eyes."[14] The masks not only conceal the identity of the subjects, but also hide any signs of emotion while they recollect horrific tales of physical and sexual abuse, suffered almost exclusively at the hands of family members. Sigmund Freud's description of trauma is pertinent if one considers the masks' function as a figurative form of protection: "We describe as 'traumatic' any excitations from outside which are powerful enough to break through the protective shield. It seems to me that the concept of trauma necessarily implies a connection of this kind of breach in an otherwise efficacious barrier against stimuli."[15] In *Trauma*, the masks symbolize the various barriers and shields — such as familial love and trust of parental, medical, or institutional authority — shattered by the actions of others.

As in *2 into 1* and *10 – 16*, Wearing encouraged everyday people to speak for themselves in *Trauma*, again reflecting Mass-Observation's ethnographic examination of the British public. The collection of information presented in *Trauma*, however, is not intended as a study or even as therapy. Though the release of these repressed feelings and stories represent, perhaps, a cathartic gesture, Wearing reveals that "the monologues are so watertight, so complete, it's as if they'd rehearsed them for the camera. But they didn't. They've probably been rehearsing them in their heads over many years."[16] Here again is ethnographic surrealism (or a surrealistic ethnography) in which the observation of human behavior is estranged from reality in a manner that reveals the failings of humanity. Wearing presents the work in a small, confessional-sized room to create a claustrophobic sense of intimacy and enclosure. The truly "disgraceful" admissions of the subjects of *Confess all on Video* and the painful recollections (often fraught with their own mixture of doubt and shame) of the subjects of *Trauma* similarly acknowledge the grim truths of modern life.

Wearing's most recent video installation, *Broad Street* (2001, jacket and pp. 2, 99 – 107, and 116), divides the viewer's attention across six projections that present scenes from a night out on Birmingham's nightclub row. Most of the footage was shot at Brannigan's, a decidedly unfashionable yet popular club attracting a wide range of older regulars and younger partygoers, all in search of drink, dancing, and either group or romantic compan-ionship. In some shots, young men check their cell phones for messages, smoke cigarettes, and survey the scene. Young women in impossibly short skirts rush down the street and into the clubs. Inside, people drink, dance, and boisterously enjoy themselves. Toward the end of the night, we see arguments, break-ups, fights, and stranded young women who must find their way home. The work takes us from the heightened anticipation of a "good night out" to that night's discouragingly frustrated conclusion. *Broad Street* is reminiscent of the Nighttown chapter of James Joyce's *Ulysses* (1922), which creates a theatrical sense of swirling activity and nightmarish circumstance in its phantasmagoric voyage through Dublin's red-light district. Just as Joyce's book turned a typical day into an epic of Odyssean consequence, *Broad Street* elevates a night in the life of the average nightclubber into an operatic display of love, lust, anger, betrayal, and abandonment.

Broad Street combines aspects of previous multiprojection video installations such as *The Unholy Three* and *Drunk* (1997 – 99, pp. 68 – 77 and 112) in its focus on loosened inhibitions, drunken behavior, and the breakdown of relationships. The primary differences between them concern people and place. *The Unholy Three* depicts differently and deeply dysfunctional characters in their personal spaces on three screens. The two men and one woman are shown engaging in weird and obsessive acts: one man comically simulates masturbation on a bed, while the lingerie-clad woman plays with an oversized champagne bottle. In the final segment of the video, the three are brought together in a pub to interact in a more polite and less desperately pathetic fashion. *Drunk* presents terminal drunks in a blank white room where their fighting, cursing, and imminent collapse into unconscious oblivion become an almost laboratory-like exercise in human observation. While the spaces in these works are either generally familiar or deliberately indeterminate, *Broad Street* shows the effect of a specific place — in particular a place for entertainment and leisure — on what could be assumed to be society's definition of mainstream or normal people. As Pedro Lapa noted in his essay on the work, "*Broad Street* reports, and it really is a report, the location of the festive ritual as it is organized by entertainment industries in contemporary societies." [17] Wearing presents nightclubbing as a form of modern human ritual, a collective activity inspired by either the desire to enjoy the company of peers or the potential for a romantic connection or sexual liaison. Nightclubs facilitate this kind of activity, with dancing (to encourage physical expressiveness and interpersonal relationships) and alcoholic beverages (to loosen or eliminate the facade of social formality). Wearing's video not only re-creates the circus atmosphere of Broad Street by visually and spatially immersing the viewer in this world, but also continues her ethnographic project by singling out this experience with its particular social and regional demographic. Her visual dissection of nightlife encapsulates the rage, ecstasy, conviviality, inebriation, and lubricity experienced in a given place in the course of a single evening.

While Gillian Wearing addresses both human comedy and tragedy in her work, the more unusual and disheartening aspects of the quotidian ultimately remain central. Her aesthetically structured techniques of ethnographic observation and representation create a picture of mundane existence that reveals human frailties without judgment, putting the onus of empathy or rejection on the viewer. The voices of a previously silent majority emerge from quickly written signs, eerily disguised faces, and the mouths of others to demonstrate the maddening impossibility of ever truly understanding the complexity of the human psyche. Wearing presents scrutinized authority, innocence corrupted by experience, masked confession and testimony, hysterical passion, and the hangover of intemperance in a manner that is painfully affecting. Crossing scientific

THE UNHOLY THREE
1995–96
Three-screen color video
projection with sound
10 minutes
Edition of 3 aside from
1 artist's proof

examination of human behavior with psychologically penetrating twists on documentary filmmaking and photography, Wearing's work holds an exacting mirror to the absurdity, ennui, and anxiety of everyday life.

NOTES

1 See Hal Foster's "The Artist as Ethnographer," in *The Return of the Real* (Cambridge, Mass: The MIT Press, 1996), pp. 171–204.

2 Norman Bryson, "Sharon Lockhart: The Politics of Inattention," *Art/Text*, no. 70 (August–October 2000), p. 57.

3 Ben Highmore, ed., *The Everyday Life Reader* (London: Routledge, 2002), p. 145.

4 James Clifford, *The Predicament of Culture: Twentieth-Century Ethnography, Literature, and Art* (Cambridge, Mass., and London: Harvard University Press, 1988), p. 143.

5 Highmore (note 3), p. 145.

6 Charles Madge and Humphrey Jennings, "They Speak for Themselves" (1936–37), in Highmore (note 3), p. 148.

7 Gillian Wearing, "Gillian Wearing in Conversation with Carl Freedman," in *Gillian Wearing* (London: Serpentine Gallery, 2000), p. 13.

8 Michel Foucault, *Discipline and Punish: The Birth of the Prison* (1976) (New York: Vintage Books, 1995), p. 170.

9 Ibid., p. 173.

10 Clifford (note 4), p. 147.

11 Ibid., p. 121.

12 Michel Foucault, *Madness and Civilization: A History of Insanity in the Age of Reason* (New York: Vintage Books, 1965), pp. 91–92.

13 Ibid., p. 100.

14 Wearing (note 7), p. 15.

15 Sigmund Freud, "Beyond the Pleasure Prinicple" (1920), in *The Freud Reader* (New York: W. W. Norton & Co., 1989), p. 607.

16 Wearing (note 7), p. 15.

17 Pedro Lapa, "A Darker Palace than Night, at Night," in *Gillian Wearing: Broad Street* (Lisbon, Portugal: Museu do Chiado, 2001), p. 13.

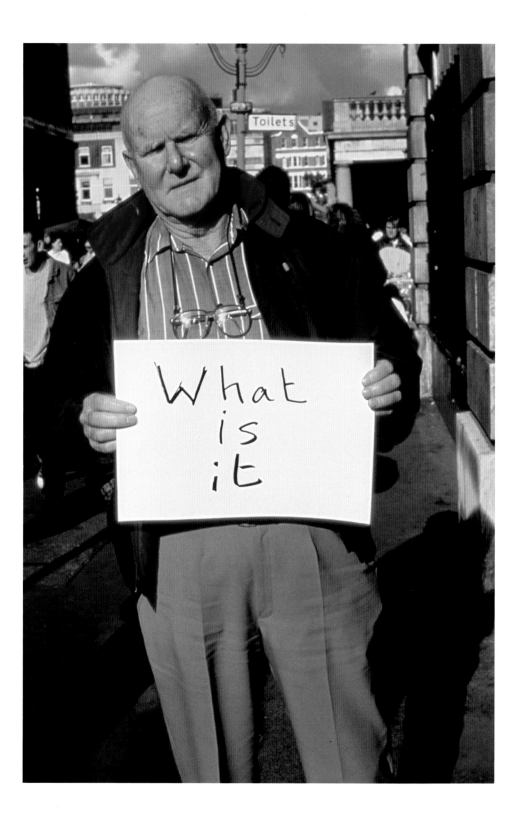

Barry Schwabsky

. . . within her someone else was hidden, one of those ferocious beings who assume a recognizable face, but with whom the you and the me come undone in a perpetually illusory dialogue.

— Maurice Blanchot,
The Most High

THE VOICE ESTRANGED

NOTHING IS MORE ALIENATING, to anyone unaccustomed to it, than hearing one's own voice played back on a tape recorder. What the apparatus records — what the objectified "others" hear — is not what resonates inside my head when I speak. The recording makes me conscious that I have no true voice. Instead, I have two voices that do not harmonize, that contradict each other: an interior voice and an exterior one. Others never hear me just as I hear myself. Moreover, this splitting of the voice, or opacity of voice to speaker, can never be directly represented. I can never communicate to another person the sound of my inner voice.

·

I wonder whether others experience this or if it's a peculiarity of my own: In my dreams, as I remember them, I never hear the sound of my own voice. The only voice I remember is that of my interlocutor. And yet — quite unlike real life, where of course I can only see myself through the intermediary of a mirror — sometimes I see myself in dreams, my observing consciousness positioned at some indeterminate objective distance from my body, a kind of hovering double.

·

In any case, it seems, my voice is not me — it corresponds neither to my image nor to itself.

SIGNS THAT SAY WHAT YOU
WANT THEM TO SAY AND
NOT SIGNS THAT SAY WHAT
SOMEONE ELSE WANTS
YOU TO SAY
1992–93
Chromogenic development
prints mounted on aluminum
Each print: 16 ½ × 12 in.
(41.9 × 30.5 cm)
Edition of 1 aside from
1 artist's proof

27

THIS ESTRANGEMENT OF THE VOICE has been one of the constant themes of Gillian Wearing's work. It is already present, at least by implication, in the first work that brought the artist to wide notice, the photographic series *Signs that say what you want them to say and not Signs that say what someone else wants you to say*. The long, unwieldy title calls a lot of attention to itself and especially to the word it repeats four times: "say." That is, although *Signs . . .* does not, like Wearing's subsequent work in video, have a sound component, it is a work about saying — but about silent saying, saying without a voice. Why would I hold up a sign in order to say something? Because you can't hear me. It's obvious that we can never hear a person in a photograph. But then why don't people in most photographs hold up signs to say what they want to say? Because photography normally "naturalizes" its own silence, asks us to let it go unnoticed. This piece makes an issue of it.

Signs . . . is one of those extremely rare artworks that has crossed over into the visual vernacular, launching a graphic device that could be instantly ripped off by the ad industry precisely because it felt so anonymous and self-evident, almost as if it had always been there — like certain popular songs. And yet we should not allow the familiarity of the work — and the simplicity of its method, its apparent artlessness — to obscure the richness of its implications. Every portrait is to some degree a collaboration between the artist and the subject, but *Signs . . .* is collaborative to a rare degree. The artist approached strangers on the street and asked them "to write down something that was in their head"[1] on sheets of standard-sized paper known in the UK as A3. If they agreed, they were then photographed holding up their inscribed *pensée*. But what is the connection between who the people seem to be and what they say they want to say? *Help, work towards world peace, I'm desperate, What is it* (no question mark), *I don't want to look like a boy, I will end this sentence but never my thoughts* — no matter how obvious the avowal may seem, one becomes immediately aware of its arbitrariness, that it was chosen from innumerable equally obvious others (let alone the others that would have been genuinely surprising), so that every banality, even the blankly tautological *me* held up by one gray-haired gent, registers as profoundly idiosyncratic. Almost any statement, one comes to feel, might have been chosen by almost any of the people Wearing photographed. They are all somehow equally revealing and unrevealing of their authors. So are they really signs that say what you want them to say and not signs that say what someone else wants you to say as their title proclaims? By printing the photographs themselves at exactly the same size as the signs they depict, Wearing established a formal parallelism between the photographs and their contents — as if to say that the photographs stand in the same relation to herself as the signs do to the people who wrote them, that the people Wearing approached had somehow given her words that she lacked. This curious little formal twist suggests that who's doing the saying depends on who is indicated by another of the title's important words, *you*. The addressee may not, after all, be the people photographed, as it first seems. As Wearing explained to the curator Donna De Salvo, "I'm more interested in how other people can put things together, how

SIGNS THAT SAY WHAT YOU
WANT THEM TO SAY AND
NOT SIGNS THAT SAY WHAT
SOMEONE ELSE WANTS
YOU TO SAY
1992–93
Chromogenic development prints
mounted on aluminum
Each print: 16 ½ × 12 in.
(41.9 × 30.5 cm)
Edition of 1 aside from
1 artist's proof

people can say something far more interesting than I can." Her very choice to become an artist was, she went on, about "attempting to express what I couldn't verbalize."[2] The work seems to imply that the very act of saying inevitably erodes the distinction between "you" and "someone else." *Je est un autre*, as the visionary poet Arthur Rimbaud maintained more than a century ago: "'I' is somebody else." We are close here, as well, to the territory of Jacques Derrida, and of his demonstration that, in the phenomenology of Edmund Husserl and in Western metaphysics in general, it is precisely the phenomenon of the voice, of speech, that excludes "the possibility of a pure and purely self-present identity."[3]

Wearing has often emphasized that her work is rooted in television more than in cinema or even in the traditions of conceptual art (by which, nonetheless, a work like *Signs . . .* is so strongly marked) or video art. For the volume on her work in the Phaidon series of contemporary art monographs, her "Artist's Choice" section consists of excerpted transcripts from Michael Apted's series of television documentaries beginning with *7 Up* (1964) — more typical choices by other artists in the series have been, say, Pascal's *Pensées*, the poetry of Anne Sexton, or the fiction of Jorge Luis Borges. She projects her undertaking as more related to documentary transcription than philosophical reflection or fictive artifice. But then philosophical reflection claims to be anchored in the real, just as fiction pretends to reflect it (a novel might be defined as a book that pretends to be a document). The most salient precursor to Wearing's work might be François Truffaut's extraordinary film about filmmaking, *Day for Night* (*La Nuit Américaine*) (1973), a tricky modernist mechanism of elusive reflexivity masquerading as a work of openhearted

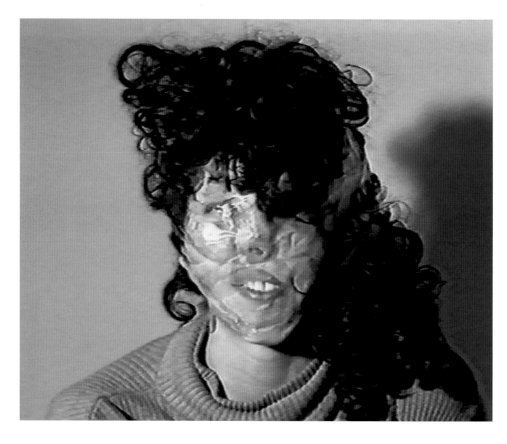

CONFESS ALL ON
VIDEO. DON'T WORRY,
YOU WILL BE IN
DISGUISE. INTRIGUED?
CALL GILLIAN.
1994
Color video with sound
30 minutes
Edition of 10 aside from
1 artist's proof

populism. In an extraordinary scene early in the movie, Séverine (Valentina Cortese), the Italian actress playing the mother in the film within the film, repeatedly flubs her lines as a scene is being filmed. She downs a glass of something between takes, trying to calm herself, and finally begs the director, "Why don't I act it out, but recite numbers instead? I always do it that way when I work with Federico" (Cortese had, of course, really worked with Fellini). "You can always post-synch my lines later, and then I'll recite your lovely dialogue, comma for comma!" "We don't do it like that here in France," the director insists; unlike the Italian cinema, in which post-synchronized sound is standard, "we record direct." [4] To separate the voice from the image would be, perhaps, to assert a Cartesian separation between soul and body.

•

Wearing's concern with just such a dualism becomes clearer in *Confess all on video. Don't worry, you will be in disguise. Intrigued? Call Gillian.* (here and p. 115). The silly masks worn by the people who responded to Wearing's ad — mostly to confess the usual sexual peccadilloes, not to mention things like the theft of a computer or putting something unpleasant in the boss's pizza — both enable the confessions and, by rendering the participants anonymous, contradict the whole idea of confession. (The anonymity of the Catholic confessional is possible because no one is anonymous in the eyes of God, a

consideration alien to the purely this-worldly ethos of Wearing's work.) The scenes are, one might say, confessional in form but only at the cost of undermining any certainty that they are confessional in content. So *Confess all . . .*, through its separation between the face and the voice, is about the possibility of confession without confession — a confession that is neither true nor false because it is authorless. *Trauma* (2000, pp. 89–93) uses the same device, starting with a newspaper ad: "Negative or traumatic experience in childhood or youth and willing to talk about it on film. Identity will be concealed." Again, the traumatic experiences are fairly banal — being beaten by one's parents, bullied at school, or sexually abused by a relative — though no less profoundly damaging for that. But this time the choice of masks — like the nature of what was to be confessed — was much more specific. As the artist has explained, "each of the masks is of an adolescent face and I wanted the masks to transport you back to this defining moment in the wearers' lives. To a time when you wouldn't have been able to see the signs yet on their faces. When they wouldn't yet have been marked by what had happened to them." [5]

•

Wearing's photographic *Self Portrait* (2000, p. 87) is linked to *Trauma* and through it to *Confess all . . .*. While the artist had scrupulously absented herself from those video works, here she lays claim to them in a different way. Like her subjects in those two pieces, she shows herself by donning a mask — again, the implication might be that, in some nonspecific way, what one has "wanted to say" in *Confess all . . .* or *Trauma* represents or substitutes for what the artist herself would have wanted to say but never does. Of course the joke is that Wearing's mask looks almost ridiculously like herself — that it's no disguise at all.

•

The impulse toward identification with a damaged individual by means of masking had previously revealed itself in Wearing's *Homage to the woman with the bandaged face who I saw yesterday down Walworth Road* (1995, pp. 32–33). In it, the artist herself impersonates the woman whom, in one of her rare first-person narratives, Wearing says she spotted on this South London street, looking quite ordinary except for her strangely "shapeless and

31

**HOMAGE TO THE WOMAN
WITH THE BANDAGED
FACE WHO I SAW YESTERDAY
DOWN WALWORTH ROAD**
1995
Black-and-white and color video
projection with subtitles
7 minutes
Edition of 3 aside from
1 artist's proof

white" profile. Only at the last minute, after Wearing had gotten into a friend's car and driven past the woman, did she realize what she had seen: "Her face was entirely covered in bandages and in a way they seemed more aesthetic than practical, like a mask."

·

It's worth dwelling for a moment on that phrase, "more aesthetic than practical" — not for what it tells us about the unknown woman behind the bandages, but for what it says about Wearing's understanding of aesthetics. She consistently emphasizes her work's links to the documentary tradition, and most of the decisions that go into it seem completely matter-of-fact. Her videos don't offer anything like Pipilotti Rist's psychedelic transports, Bill Viola's sublime transports, or Stan Douglas's cerebral gamesmanship. That is, they don't emphasize their own stylistic resources, let alone their constant slippages between reality and invention. All the decisions that go into the work come across as primarily practical ones. But *Homage to the woman . . .* clues us in to the way Wearing sees choices that others might make on a practical basis as, in fact, aesthetic decisions. In that sense, Wearing is much closer to the sober, deadpan style of early conceptual art and the first wave of video art that followed than she is to the more baroque approaches to video that have emerged since the 1980s. Above all, the decision to use masks in *Confess all . . .* and *Trauma* — on one level a profoundly practical decision to help people feel comfortable telling their secrets by assuring them, more certainly than if they were simply *promised* that their faces would later be blacked out, that they would not be identified — was the most profoundly stylistic of decisions, and one that furthermore allows us to reflect on the strangely fictive nature of even the most intimate communication.

·

The focus on childhood and adolescence that distinguishes *Trauma* from *Confess all . . .* links the former with two extraordinary works from 1997, *10 – 16* (pp. 18 – 19 and 55 – 59) and *2 into 1* (pp. 47 – 53). In these works, Wearing dissociates the speaker and his voice in an even more extreme and disturbing way: In these works the "mask" is, so to speak, the entire body. The conventions of the talking-heads documentary that *Confess all . . .* and *Trauma* evoke and ultimately erode come under more concerted assault in *10 – 16* and *2 into 1*. In the former, we hear a series of "confessions" by children and adolescents within the age span described by the work's title, ranging from an innocuous account of the pleasures of riding buses around London to the more alarming reflections of a child who says of his mother, "I'd love to kill her very much, as I found out she is a lesbian."[6] But what one sees is a sequence of adult actors lip-synching the kids' words. It's obvious that *this* voice could not belong to *this* body — there's no illusionism involved — and yet there is an uncanny "rightness" to the matching of the two, so that one feels completely disoriented with regard to the possible truth or falsehood, authenticity or fictiveness of the monologues. And this feeling of uncertainty intensifies the emotional force of the disclosures: What touches us is not so much that the feelings expressed *are* real — we know that their truth is unknowable — as the more abstract or notional recognition that they *could be* real. Possibility trumps fact. To hear a boy's voice emerging from a man's body to say, "I feel like I'm a man in a boy's body" is disconcerting precisely because it becomes so hard to grasp the difference between a man in a boy's body and a boy in a man's body — hard, therefore, to grasp the difference (which the work itself seems to depend on) between manhood and boyhood.

•

MY FAVOURITE TRACK
(detail and installation view),
1994
Five-monitor color video
installation with sound
90 minutes
Edition of 1 aside from
1 aritst's proof

The more compact and intense *2 into 1* uses a similar technique of lip-synching. This time there are just three heads, three voices, and they are knit into a single situation. From a woman's mouth we hear the voices of her two sons as they talk about her; from the sons' mouths, we hear their mother's opinions of them. Since these are not, apparently, professional actors, the technical challenge of matching voices to faces must have been much greater than in *10–16*. More importantly, this work projects the estrangement of the voice and the dislocation of identity beyond the comforts of anonymity; it demands

the collaboration of a family in Wearing's play with the tensions of their own emotional entanglement. As the mother says — or rather, as one of the sons says in the mother's voice — "Having children brings out two very, very extreme emotions in us, which is that one's constantly faced with the border of love and hate." Two into one, indeed. Works like *Signs . . .* , *Confess all . . .* , *10–16*, and *Trauma* — or even *Homage to the woman . . .* — are all essentially variations on the idea of portraiture. The same is also true of other key early works like *Dancing in Peckham* (1994, p. 13) — Wearing's most straightforward self-portrait, and an interesting inversion of her usual theme of dissociating voice and visage; in this video she is seen dancing to an unheard beat. That beat existed only in Wearing's head, but in *My Favourite Track* she shows other people singing as they listen to Walkmans — devices that make manifest the divide between the inner voice and outer voice: it's impossible to sing in tune when your Walkman is cranked up, because you can't hear your voice at all. If hearing your own voice on a tape recorder causes a form of alienating self-consciousness, this creates the comparable form of alienated unself-consciousness. "Listening to it," as the artist has remarked of *My Favourite Track*, "is like being in a tower of Babel, where everyone is talking at once but no one is listening to anyone else. The piece is about isolation."[7] In *2 into 1*, as in the video *Sacha and Mum* (1996, pp. 20–21), portraiture expands into the realm of group portraiture — which Wearing had broached less successfully as early as 1993 in the series of photographs called *Take Your Top Off*, in each of which the artist is seen holding the shutter-release as she portrays herself together in bed with a male-to-female transsexual, both of them naked from the waist up. In this case, the ambiguous gender status of the artist's bedfellows is another marker of the inner split that has preoccupied her — and one can imagine a disjunction between voice and appearance here as well — though she has not managed to give this a vivid formal manifestation as she has in much of her other work (just as her tacit identification with the subjects of her portraiture perhaps becomes too patent here). Portraits of isolation though these works may be, the serial nature of many of them — most spectacularly *Signs . . .* , with approximately 600 images — also makes them group portraits of a sort. There is a collective subject being approached here, which is why critic Michael Newman has been able to treat Wearing's work as a "demotic art," an exemplar of "a certain kind of savvy, street-aware art that wants to claim a place for itself in popular culture, and engage with the everyday lives of 'ordinary' people."[8] Wearing herself once described the effect of showing the *Signs . . .* "en masse" as a "kind of democracy."[9]

Recently, however, Wearing seems to have become more and more interested in something that could hardly be engaged by means of this serial individualism, namely the dynamics of large groups — "mass observation," as this particular exhibition would have it. Her 1996 video projection *Sixty Minute Silence* (pp. 10 and 43–45), otherwise rather a one-off in the development of Wearing's work, might be a sort of dress rehearsal for this incipient engagement with group portraiture. The twenty-six figures who stand or sit through this mural-like, nearly static work — viewers have mistaken the piece for a slide projection until they notice the subtle movements of subjects trying to force themselves to keep still for so long — are not, as they appear to be, police officers; they are just dressed that way. The uniform is a different kind of mask, a fiction of social identity. (Wearing has said of *Signs . . .* , "the white of the paper of the signs became like a uniform."[10]) But Wearing's major work of group portraiture so far has been the three-channel video installation *Drunk* (1997–99, pp. 68–77 and 112), about a group of local inebriates the artist filmed in her studio. In this work, it might seem, there has been no device (no signs, no lip-synching, no masks, no uniforms) interposed to formalize and distance the embarrassment of self-disclosure — it is just the stark exposure of a tragic human condition and a refractory social problem. Perhaps, in the final instance, the white backdrop against which *Drunk* was acted functions as a minimal form of self-distancing

TAKE YOUR TOP OFF
1993
Chromogenic development
prints
Three parts, each: 28 ¾ × 39 in.
(73 × 99.1 cm)
Edition of 3 aside from
1 artist's proof

(like the bright blue background of *Trauma* but also "the white of the paper" in *Signs* . . .). But it's more, I think, that alcohol itself functions as a sort of internal mask or uniform, a way of distancing oneself from oneself. Alcohol, more than that white sheet, is the backdrop that erases the "real" scene of the artist's studio against which the work's action takes place. I am reminded of the anthropologist and psychologist Gregory Bateson's observation that "the 'sobriety' of the alcoholic is characterized by an unusually disastrous variant of the Cartesian dualism, the division between Mind and Matter." [11] It is this faulty sobriety that the drinking tries to cure. So the group portrait *Drunk* concerns, in this sense, the very same dualism within individual identity as Wearing's individual portraits did.

In England, where drinking to get drunk is a more common and socially acceptable behavior among people who do not consider themselves alcoholics than in many other societies, alcoholism as a social problem undoubtedly takes on forms that are more subtle, precisely because they are more pervasive, than they might be elsewhere. Wearing's newest major video installation, *Broad Street* (2001, jacket and pp. 2, 99–107, and 116), is not overtly about alcoholism in the way that *Drunk* is, but it is certainly about a form of social existence that is organized around the rituals of drinking as a way of getting outside of oneself, and thus it is not surprising that as the Portuguese curator Pedro Lapa has said, the work's multitude of simultaneous sights and sounds results in a "plurality of stimuli that tend to disassociate the sound from the vision" [12] — the same disassociation that has been the trope for the tragic separation of body and soul in Wearing's work from the beginning. Here it takes a form that is perhaps closer to that of *My Favourite Track* than to any of her other previous works. Although Wearing has been working in an almost systematic fashion toward the collective subject that is revealed in *Broad Street*, she has always approached this through an essentially existential basis, the malaise of the individual's divided soul.

I CAN NEVER FORGET THAT I AM ALWAYS "OUTSIDE" the inner experience of another person. Wearing adds to this knowledge the less obvious observation that talking about such experiences — communicating them to each other — also places the other person outside of his or her own experience, introducing an irreducible inner difference or nonidentity. We share our self-estrangement by giving voice to it. Cold comfort.

NOTES

1   Quoted in Andrew Graham-Dixon, "Wearing Masks," *Vogue* (UK) (September 2000), p. 140.

2   Quoted in "Donna De Salvo in Conversation with Gillian Wearing," in Russell Ferguson, Donna De Salvo, and John Slyce, *Gillian Wearing* (London: Phaidon, 1999), p. 11.

3   Jacques Derrida, *Speech and Phenomena and Other Essays on Husserl's Theory of Signs*, trans. David B. Allison (Evanston, Ill.: Northwestern University Press, 1973), p. 83.

4   François Truffaut, *Day for Night*, trans. Sam Flores (New York: Grove Press, 1975), pp. 55–56.

5   Quoted in "Gillian Wearing in Conversation with Carl Freedman," in Juan Vincente Aliaga, Marta Gili, and Carl Freedman, *Gillian Wearing* (Madrid: Fundación "la Caixa," 2001), English text unpag., Spanish trans. p. 28.

6   Quotations from transcripts of texts of *10–16* and *2 into 1* are from Ferguson et al. (note 2), pp. 136–143.

7   Quoted in "Donna De Salvo in Conversation with Gillian Wearing," (note 2), p. 21.

8   Michael Newman, "The Demotic Art of Gillian Wearing," *Parachute* 102 (2001), p. 98, French trans. p. 99.

9   Quoted in "Donna De Salvo in Conversation with Gillian Wearing," (note 2), p. 11.

10 Ibid., p. 12.

11 Gregory Bateson, "The Cybernetics of 'Self': A Theory of Alcoholism," in *Steps to an Ecology of Mind* (London: Granada Publishing, 1973), p. 284.

12 Pedro Lapa, "A Darker Place than Night, at Night," in *Gillian Wearing: Broad Street* (Lisbon: Museu do Chiado, 2001), p. 5.

PLATES

SIXTY MINUTE SILENCE

SIXTY MINUTE SILENCE
1996
Color video projection with
sound
60 minutes
Edition of 1 aside from 1
artist's proof
Collection of Anthony T.
Podesta, Washington, D.C.

PAGE 43: INSTALLATION VIEW
PAGES 44–45: DETAIL

2 INTO 1

2 INTO 1

1997
Color video with sound
4 minutes, 30 seconds
Edition 2 of 5
Collection of Eileen
and Peter Norton,
Santa Monica, Calif.

PAGES 47–53

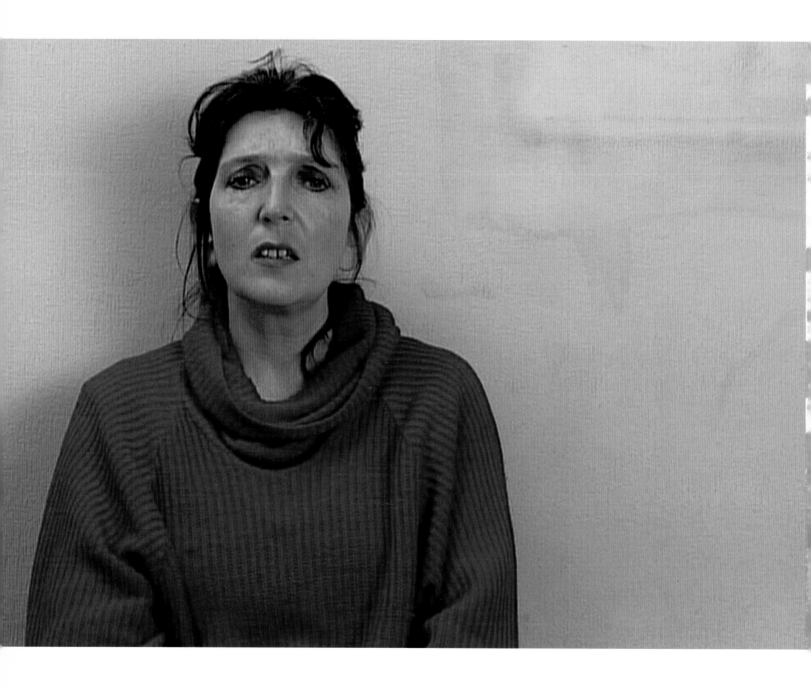

10–16

10 – 16
1997
Color video projection
with sound
15 minutes
Edition of 3 aside from
1 artist's proof

PAGES 55–59

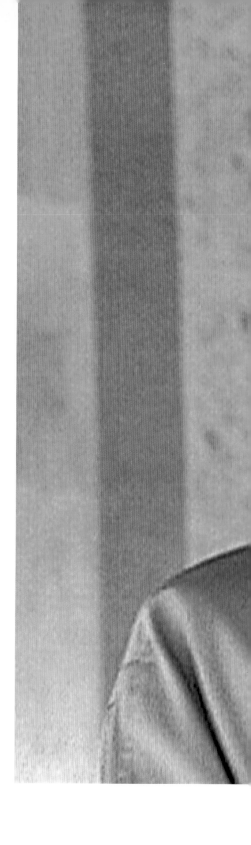

we went togetheR properly foR 5 maths and on and off oveR Time IN fairness se talks Behind my BACk Like That I am useless IN Bed. I am A Two timeR and now she thinks I am Fucking grass. She shiT ryder she only does one pasition and she falls asleep after five mintues she useless. She don't know what She is doing you got her to Tell her what to do. Like Turn side wAys and open your Legs wide and start going. or Turn Back Like dog. and do The Back wAy. She Been one of my mates Behind my Back and she told me that he raped me and I asked him and he said No I Belived him what he said she also told me she was dieing of Aids and canceR and Liver dieseas and she was pregnant She told me she Been with otheR Blokes Behind my Back if I did not stay with her she got her mates to do me in. she got couple of her mates To do me By saying that I hiT heR. She was dangeous By throwing The funiture around and smash my windows when she is drunk she shouts at me and

get me aBusement aBout nothing. she smashed one of my mates FLAT BecuSe She was a ponch. and She ponch of my mates To get a drink she turn ap at the post office To see if any one has Been paid. and then she turns violent and Start to steal money off the people till they are skint. and goes and starts again. Then you don't see her foR few days she going to see other mates or don't see her on her payday. she Looks around to sleep some were Like one of my mates in the area and start trouble there. and she a tant she sleep with anyone who's got house or aload of money. when She is SobeR she clean the house up make sure everything clear and tidy.

THERESA AND ALI
1998
Chromogenic
development prints
Diptych, each: 20 × 20 in.
(50.8 × 50.8 cm)
Edition of 5 aside from 1
artist's proof

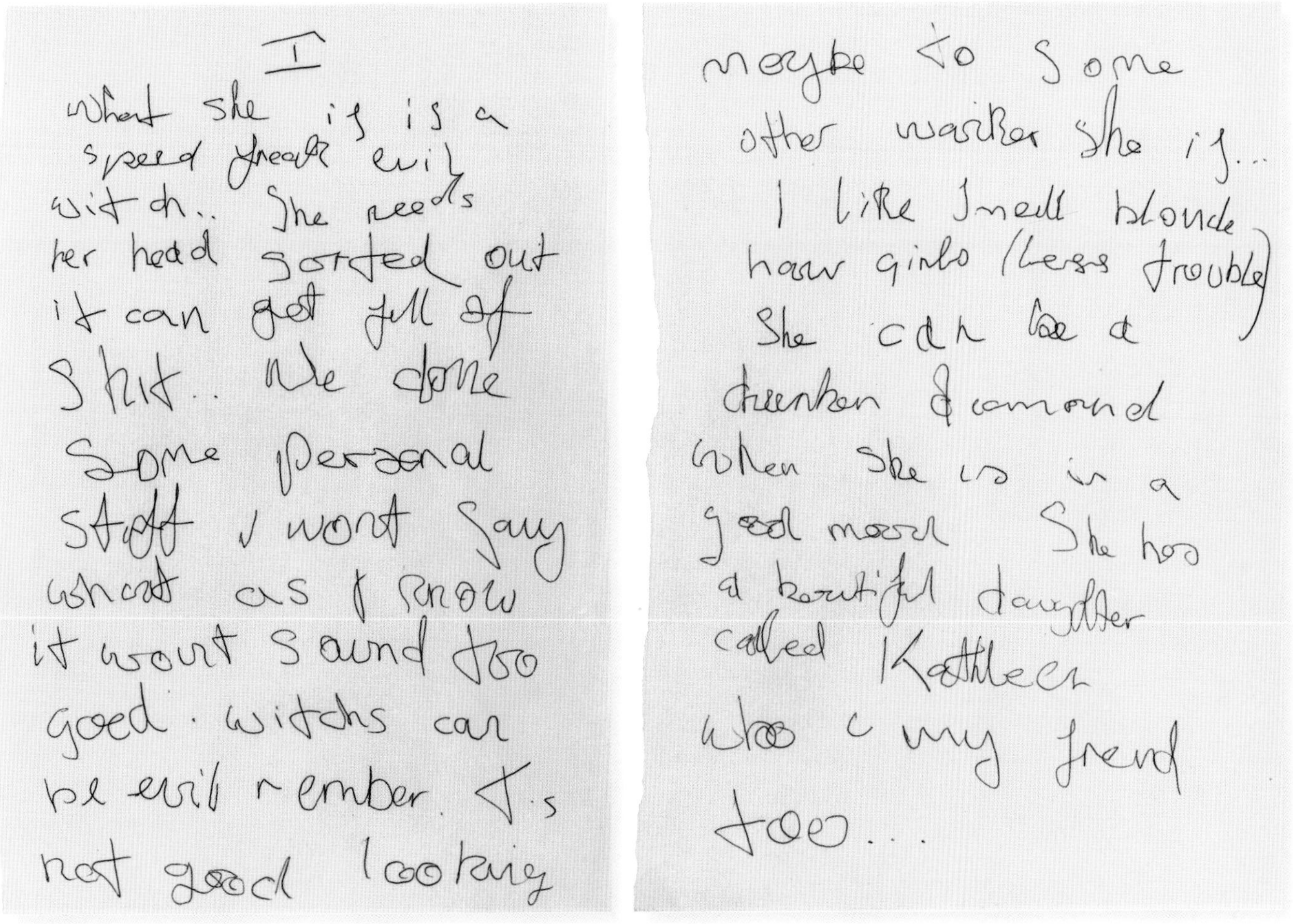

I

what she is is a
speed freak evil
witch.. She needs
her head sorted out
it can get full of
shit.. We done
some personal
stuff I wont say
what as I know
it wont sound too
good. witchs can
be evil rember. J.s
not good looking

maybe to some
other worker she is...
I like small blonde
hair girls (Less trouble)
She can be a
drunken diamond
when she is in a
good mood. She has
a beautiful daughter
called Kathleen
who I my frend
too...

THERESA AND BEN
1998
Chromogenic
development prints
Diptych, each: 20 × 20 in.
(50.8 × 50.8 cm)
Edition of 5 aside from 1
artist's proof

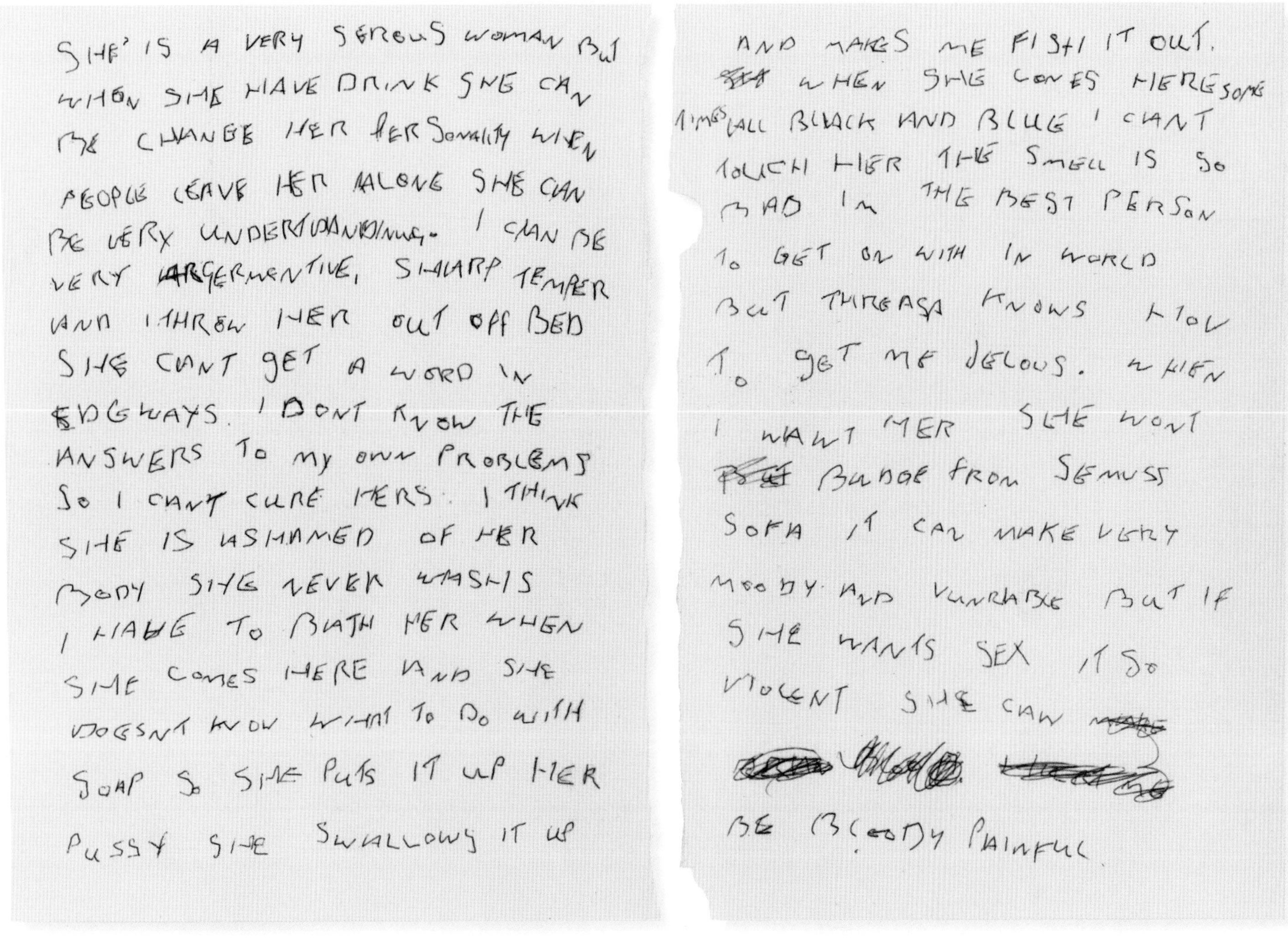

SHE IS A VERY SERIOUS WOMAN BUT WHEN SHE HAVE DRINK SHE CAN BE CHANGE HER PERSONALITY WHEN PEOPLE LEAVE HER ALONE SHE CAN BE VERY UNDERSTANDING. I CAN BE VERY ~~ARGERMENTIVE~~ SHARP TEMPER AND I THREW HER OUT OFF BED SHE CANT GET A WORD IN EDGWAYS. I DONT KNOW THE ANSWERS TO MY OWN PROBLEMS SO I CANT CURE HERS. I THINK SHE IS ASHAMED OF HER BODY SHE NEVER WASHIS I HAVE TO BATH HER WHEN SHE COMES HERE AND SHE DOESNT KNOW WHAT TO DO WITH SOAP SO SHE PUTS IT UP HER PUSSY SHE SWALLOWS IT UP

AND MAKES ME FISH IT OUT. ~~SHE~~ WHEN SHE COMES HERE SOME TIMES ALL BLACK AND BLUE I CANT TOUCH HER THE SMELL IS SO BAD IM THE BEST PERSON TO GET ON WITH IN WORLD BUT THREASA KNOWS HOW TO GET ME JELOUS. WHEN I WANT HER SHE WONT ~~FOR~~ BUDGE FROM SEMUSS SOFA IT CAN MAKE VERY MOODY AND VUNRABLE BUT IF SHE WANTS SEX IT SO VIOLENT SHE CAN ~~~~ BE BLOODY PAINFUL.

THERESA AND GEORGE
1998
Chromogenic
development prints
Diptych, each: 20 × 20 in.
(50.8 × 50.8 cm)
Edition of 5 aside from 1
artist's proof

FORM MY POINT OF VIEW SHE iS
ABSOLAUTELY STUPID. SHE DOSE NOT
RESPECT HERSELF. i MEAN. ANYONE
WHO SELLS THEMSELVES FOR ACAN
OF BEER HAS GOT TO STUPID
ADD. FOR A START NOT APPERING
IN CORT WHEN DUE SHE THINKS
SHE ABOVE THE LAW. NOW SHE iS
SEEING MICK AND I KNOW SHE
is going TO A BURNED HE EVEN SAID
LAST NIGHT HE WANTED TO DUMP HER AT
MY PLACE. YET LAST WEEK HE
ASKED HER TO MARRY HER iF SHE
WANTED A CAN OF BEER THATS
iT. i TOLD HER YOU CANT KEEP DOING
THIS AS YOU WILL GET A A DISEASE BUT AS
LONG AS SHE HAS GOT A CAN OF
BEER IN HER HAND SHE COULDENT
CARE LESS. WE HAVE SEXUAL
RELATIONSHIPS. AS SHE HAS A GOOD
HART. AND A GOOD SENCE OF HOUMOUR

BUT SHE iS. OWERWEIGHT. ADD HAS
NO SENCE OF DREES AS LONG AS
YOU ARE WITH TRESA YOU ARE NEVE
SHORT OF PILLOW. YOU CAN USE
HER BRESTS

THERESA AND SEAMUS
1992
Chromogenic
development prints
Diptych, each: 20 × 20 in.
(50.8 × 50.8 cm)
Edition of 5 aside from
1 artist's proof

DRUNK

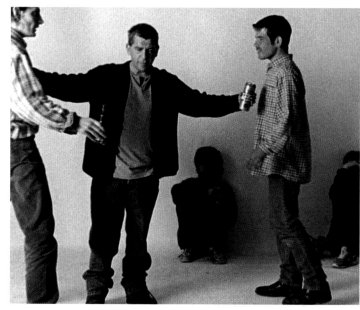

DRUNK
1997–99
Three-screen black-and-white
video projection with sound
23 minutes
Edition of 5 aside from
1 artist's proof
Courtesy of Maureen Paley
Interim Art, London, and
Gorney Bravin + Lee,
New York

PAGES 68–77

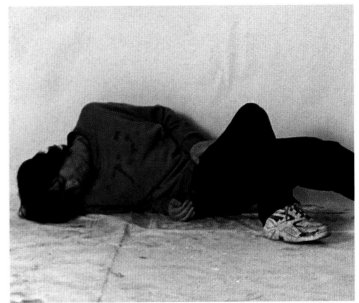

I LOVE YOU

I LOVE YOU
1999
Color video projection with sound
60 minutes
Edition 2 of 5
Goetz Collection, Munich

PAGES 79–85

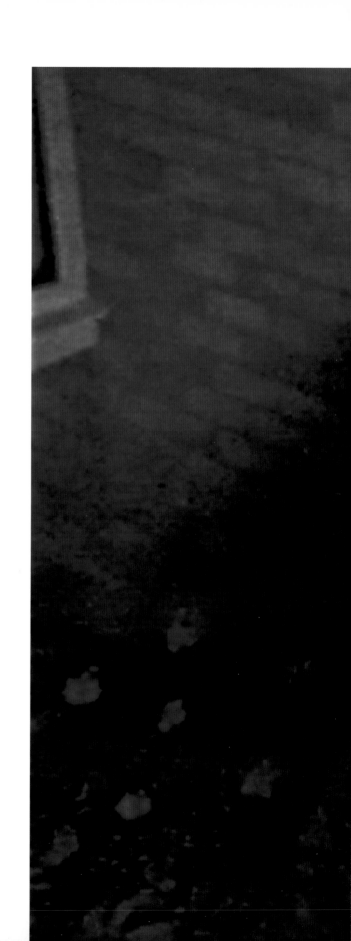

SELF PORTRAIT

SELF PORTRAIT
2000
Chromogenic development print
68 × 68 in. (172.7 × 172.7 cm)
Edition 9 of 10
Private collection

TRAUMA

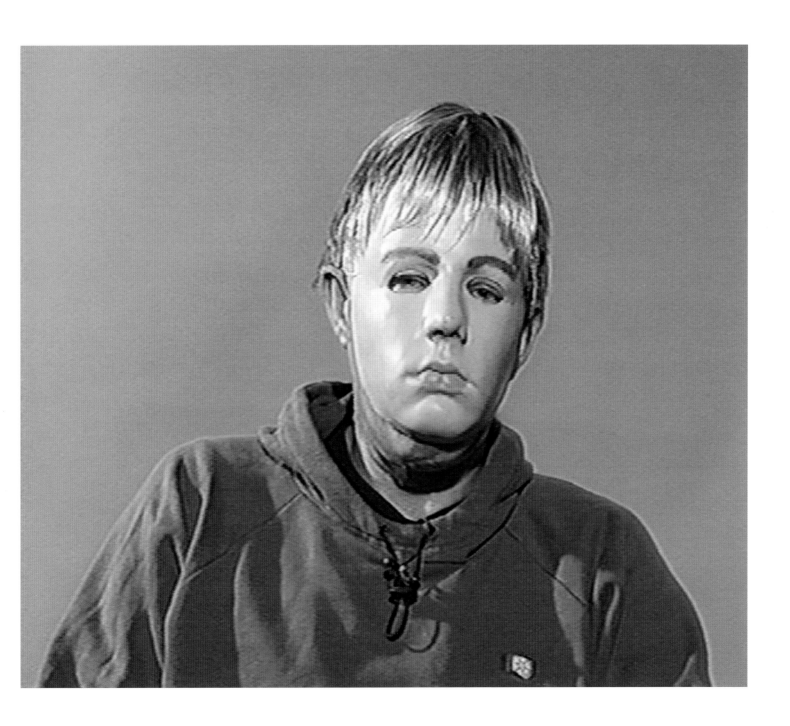

TRAUMA
2000
Rear-projection color video
projection with sound
30 minutes
Edition 2 of 5
Collection of Musée d'Art
Moderne de la Ville de
Paris, Paris

PAGES 89–93

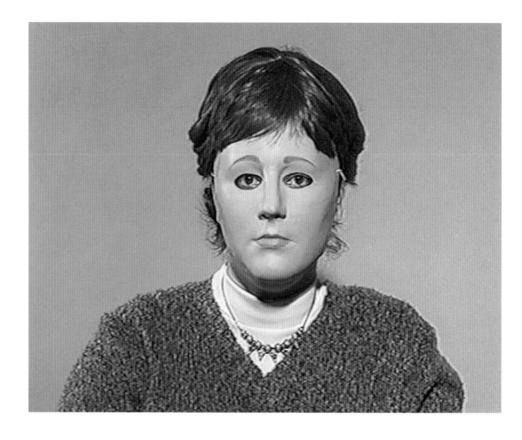

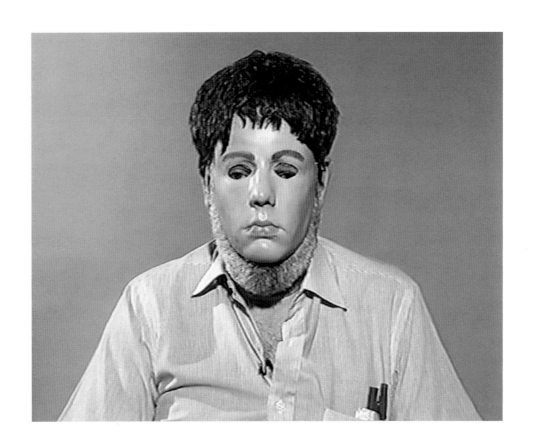

PRELUDE

PRELUDE
2000
Black-and-white video
projection with sound
4 minutes
Edition of 5 aside from
2 artist's proofs

PAGES 95–97

96

BROAD STREET

BROAD STREET
2001
Six-screen color video
projection with sound
40 minutes
Edition of 2 aside from
2 artist's proofs

PAGES 99–107

Born 1963 Birmingham,
United Kingdom
Lives and works in London

EDUCATION

1985–87 Chelsea School of Art, B. Tech
Art and Design

1987–1990 Goldsmith's College, University
of London B.A. (Hons.) Fine Art

AWARDS

1993 BT Young Contemporaries

1997 Turner Prize 1997

1998 For *2 into 1*

Oberhausen Short Film Festival

Prize of the Ministry of
Employment, Social Affairs and
Urban Development, Culture
and Sport

2000 British Television Advertising
Awards

Public Service: Gold

SOLO EXHIBITIONS

1993 City Racing, London

1994 Maureen Paley Interim Art, London

1996 *Gillian Wearing, City Projects —
Prague, Part II*, The British
Council, Prague (catalogue)

Le Consortium, Dijon, France

Maureen Paley Interim Art, London

Valentina Moncada, Rome
(British Council) (catalogue)

Wish You Were Here (Video Evenings
at De Appel), Amsterdam

1997 Emi Fontana, Milan

Galerie Drantmann, Brussels, Belgium

Jay Gorney Modern Art, New York

Kunsthaus Zürich, Switzerland
(catalogue)

10–16, Chisenhale Gallery, London

Wiener Secession, Vienna (catalogue)

1998 Centre d'Art Contemporain,
Geneva, Switzerland

Gallery Koyanagi, Tokyo

1999 *Drunk*, De Vleeshal, Middelburg,
Netherlands

Galerie Anne de Villepoix, Paris

Maureen Paley Interim Art, London

2000 Gorney Bravin + Lee, New York

Regen Projects, Los Angeles

Serpentine Gallery, London
(catalogue)

2001 Centro Galego de Arte
Contemporánea, Santiago, Spain

Fundación "la Caixa," Madrid
(catalogue)

Gillian Wearing: Broad Street, Museo
do Chiado, Lisbon (catalogue)

Gillian Wearing: Sous Influence,
Musée d'Art Moderne de la
Ville de Paris, Paris (catalogue)

Unspoken, Kunstverein München,
Munich

2002 Kunsthaus Glarus, Glarus,
Switzerland

Maureen Paley Interim Art, London
Gillian Wearing: A Trilogy, Vancouver
Art Gallery, Vancouver (catalogue)

GROUP EXHIBITIONS

1991   *Clove 1*, The Clove Building, London

Empty Gestures, Diorama Art Centre, London

Piece Talks, Diorama Art Centre, London

1992   *British Art Group Show*, Le Musée des Beaux Arts dans Le Havre, France

Instruction, Marconi Gallery, Milan

1993   *BT Young Contemporaries*, Cornerhouse, Manchester, England; Orchard Gallery, Derry, Northern Ireland; The Maplin Art Gallery, Sheffield, England; City Museum and Art Gallery, Stoke-on-Trent, England; Centre for Contemporary Art, Glasgow, Glasgow (catalogue)

Mandy Loves Declan 100%, Mark Boote Gallery, New York

Okay Behaviour, 303 Gallery, New York

2 into 1, Centre 181 Gallery, London

Vox Pop, Laure Genillard Gallery, London

1994   *Domestic Violence*, curated by Alison Jacques, Gio Marconi's House, Milan

Fuori Fase, Via Farini, Milan

Le Shuttle, Künstlerhaus Bethanien, Berlin (catalogue)

Not Self-Portrait, Karsten Schubert, London

R.A.S., curated by Gianni Romano, Galerie Analix B & L Polla, Geneva (catalogue)

3.016.026, Theoretical Events, Naples

Uncertain Identity, Galerie Analix B & L Polla, Geneva (catalogue)

1995   *Aperto '95*, Nouveau Musée, Institut d'Art Contemporain, Villeurbanne, France

Brilliant! New Art from London, Walker Art Center, Minneapolis (catalogue)

Brill: Works on Paper by Brilliant Artists, Montgomerie Glasgoe Fine Art, Minneapolis

British Art Show 4, Upper Campfield Market, Manchester, England; Collective Gallery, Edinburgh; Ffotogallery, Cardiff, Wales (catalogue)

Campo, Forty-Sixth Biennale di Venezia, Venice, Italy

Gone, Blum & Poe, Santa Monica, Calif.

Hello! Andréhn-Schiptjenko, Stockholm

Hotel Mama (Aperto '95), Kunstraum, Vienna

It's Not a Picture, Galleria Emi Fontana, Milan

Make Believe, Royal College of Art, London (catalogue)

Mobius Strip, Basilico Fine Arts, New York (catalogue)

Mysterium Alltag, Kampnagel, Hamburg, Germany

Sage, Galerie Michel Rien, Tours, France

X/Y, Musée National d'Art Moderne, Centre Georges Pompidou, Paris

1996   *a/drift: Scenes From the Penetrable Culture*, Center for Curatorial Studies, Bard College, New York (catalogue)

The Aggression of Beauty, Galerie Arndt & Partner, Berlin

Auto-reverse 2, Centre National d'Art Contemporain Grenoble, France

The Cauldron, Henry Moore Institute, Leeds, England (catalogue)

Electronic Undercurrents: Art and Video in Europe, Statens Museum für Kunst, Copenhagen (catalogue)

The Fifth New York Video Festival, The Film Society of Lincoln Center, New York

Full House: Young British Art,
Kunstmuseum Wolfsburg, Germany
(catalogue)

I.D., Stedelijk Van Abbemuseum,
Eindhoven, Netherlands (catalogue)

Imagined Communities, Oldham Art
Gallery; John Hansard Gallery,
Southampton, England; Firstsite,
Colchester, England; Walsall
Museum and Art Gallery;
Royal Festival Hall, London;
Gallery of Modern Art, Glasgow,
Scotland (catalogue)

Life/Live, Musée d'art Moderne
de la Ville de Paris, Paris (catalogue)

NowHere, Louisiana Museum of
Modern Art, Humlebaek, Denmark
(catalogue)

*Pandemonium; London Festival of
Moving Images*, Institute of
Contemporary Arts, London

Playpen & Corpus Delirium, Kunsthalle
Zürich, Switzerland (catalogue)

Private View, Contemporary Art in
the Bowes Museum, Barnard Castle,
County Durham, organized by the
Henry Moore Institute (catalogue)

Toyama Now '96, The Museum of
Modern Art, Toyama, Japan (catalogue)

Traffic, CAPC Musée Contemporain
Bordeaux, France (catalogue)

1997 Galerie Anne de Villepoix, Paris

Gillian Wearing/Barbara Visser,
Bloom Gallery, Amsterdam

I.D., Nouveau Musée, Villeurbanne,
France

*In Visible Light: Photography and
Classification in Art, Science, and
the Everyday*, Museum of
Modern Art, Oxford (catalogue)

*Package Holiday — New British Art in
the Ophiuchus Collection*, The Hydra
Workshop, Hydra, Greece

Pictura Britannica: Art from Britain,
Museum of Contemporary Art,
Sydney, Australia; Adelaide,
Australia; Wellington, New Zealand

Private Face — Urban Space,
coorganized by the Hellenic Art
Galleries Association and
The Rethymnon Centre for
Contemporary Art, Athens
and Rethymnon, Greece

Projects, The Irish Museum of
Modern Art, Dublin (catalogue)

Sensation, Saatchi Collection, Royal
Academy of Art, London (catalogue)

S. L. Simpson Gallery, Toronto

Splash, AAC Galerie Weimar, Germany

Tales from the City, Stills Gallery,
Edinburgh (catalogue)

The Turner Prize 1997, Tate
Gallery, London (catalogue)

1998 *A Collection in the Making*, The Irish
Museum of Modern Art, Dublin
(catalogue)

Contemporary British Art, The Museum
of Contemporary Art, Seoul, Korea
(catalogue)

ENGLISH ROSE in Japan, The
Ginza Artspace, Tokyo

Fast Forward Body Check, Kunstverein,
Hamburg

Galerija Dante Marino Cettina,
Umag, Croatia

*Internationale Foto Triennale/Photography
as Concept*, Galerien der Stadt Esslingen,
Esslingen, Germany (catalogue)

In Visible Light, Moderna Museet,
Stockholm

La Concienza Luccicante, Palazzo
delle Esposizioni, Rome

La Sphere de L'Intime, Le Printemps
de Cahors, Saint-Cloud, France

DRUNK
1997–99
3-screen black-and-white
video projection with sound
23 minutes
Edition of 5 aside from
1 artist's proof

Made in London, Musea de Electricidade, Lisbon

Musée du Rochechouart, Rochechouart, France

Real/Life: New British Art, Japanese Museum Tour, Tochigi Prefectural Museum of Fine Arts; Fukuoka City Art Museum; Hiroshima Museum of Contemporary Art; Tokyo Museum of Contemporary Art (catalogue)

UK Maximum Diversity, Galerie Krinzinger, Bregenz and Künste Wien, Vienna

Videorama, Depot, Kunst und Diskussion, Vienna

White Noise, Kunsthalle Berne, Switzerland (catalogue)

1999   *Common People*, Fondazione Sandretto re Rebaudengo per l'Arte, Turin, Italy (catalogue)

Ex-Change, La Criee, Centre d'Art Contemporain, Rennes, France

Garden of Eros, Centre Cultural Tecla Sala, Barcelona

Hundstage, Gesellschaft für Aktuelle Kunst, Bremen, Germany

La Coscienza Luccicante, Palazzo delle Esposizioni, Rome

People, Le Spot, Contemporary Art Centre, Le Havre, France

Private Room/Public Space, Almeers Centrum Hedendaagse Kunst, Al Almere, Netherlands

Rattling the Frame: The Photographic Space 1974–1999, SF Camerawork, San Francisco

Rewind to the Future, Bonner Kunstverein, Bonn, and Neue Berliner Kunstverein, Berlin

Searchlight: Consciousness at the Millennium, The California College of Arts and Crafts, Oakland (catalogue)

6th International Istanbul Biennale, Istanbul, Turkey (catalogue)

Sweetie: Female Identity in British Video, The British School at Rome

This Other World of Ours, TV Gallery, Moscow

The Viewing Room, Kansas City Art Institute, Kansas City, Mo.

2000   *Autowerke*, Deichtorhallen, Hamburg

Contemporary Art Center, Cincinnati, Ohio

docudrama, Bury St. Edmunds Art Gallery, Bury St. Edmunds, England

Intelligence: New British Art 2000, Tate Britain, London (catalogue)

Let's Entertain, Walker Art Center, Minneapolis (catalogue)

Makeshift, ArtPace, San Antonio, Tex.

Puerile '69, The Living Art Museum, Reykjavík, Iceland

Quotidiana, Castello di Rivoli, Turin, Italy

Sydney Biennale, Museum of Contemporary Art, Sydney, Australia (catalogue)

Tate Britain Collection, Tate Gallery, London

Tate Modern Collection, Tate Modern, London

2001   *ABBILD Recent Portraiture and Depiction*, Landemuseum Joanneum, Graz, Austria

Biennale de Lyon Art Contemporain 2001, Lyon, France (catalogue)

Birmingham, Ikon Gallery, Birmingham

Century City, Tate Modern, London (catalogue)

Confidence pour confidence, Casino Luxembourg, Luxembourg

Film Festival Rotterdam, Museum Boijmans Van Beuningen, Rotterdam, Netherlands

Inner State of Health: The Person in the Mirror of Contemporary Art, Kunstmuseum Liechtenstein

Milano Europa 2001, Palazzo della Triannale, Milan

No World without You: Reflections of Identity in New British Art, Herzliya Museum of Art, Tel Aviv

Telling Tales: Narrative Impulses in Recent Art, Tate Liverpool, England

Video Evidence, Southampton City Art Gallery, Southampton, England

2002 *Acquisitions 2001 — Part 1: Photographs, Video Installations, Video*, National Museum of Contemporary Art, Athens

Bienal de São Paulo, Brazil (catalogue)

I Promise It's Political, Museum Ludwig, Cologne (catalogue)

Remix: Contemporary Art and Pop Music, Tate Liverpool, England (catalogue)

The Video Show, Centraal Museum, Utrecht, Netherlands

OTHER PROJECTS

1994 Holly Street Estate Art Project, London

Rooseum Video Programme, Rooseum Center for Contemporary Art, Sweden

1995 *Western Security*, Hayward Gallery Foyer, London

1996 Guest editor, *Documents sur l'art*

1998 *Expanding Pictures*, BBC2

South Bank Show, London Weekend Television

BIBLIOGRAPHY

1992 Raphael, Amy. "Hype: Write to Reply." *The Face*, no. 51 (December).

1993 Archer, Michael. "O Camera, O Mores." *Art Monthly*, no. 166 (May), pp. 14–16.

Feaver, William. "Treasures in the Wendy House of the Lost Boys." *Observer*, July 4, p. 59.

Graham-Dixon, Andrew. "That Way Madness Lies." *Independent*, June 22.

Guha, Tania. "Gillian Wearing: City Racing." *Time Out* (March 24–31).

Milner, Catherine. "Positive Exposure for New Talent." *Times*, February 27.

Stallabass, Julian. "Power to the People." *Art Monthly*, no. 165 (April), pp. 15–17.

1994 Craddock, Sacha. "Great British Hopes: Rising Stars in the Arts Firmament." *Times*, June 14.

Currah, Mark. *Time Out* (June 29–July 6), p. 50.

Harpers Magazine 288, no. 1728, p. 21.

Jaio, Miren. "Cinco Artistas Inglesas: Voces En El Espacio." *Lapiz*, no. 106 (October/November), pp. 12–19.

Lillington, David. "Real Life in London." *Paletten*, no. 219 (April), p. 12.

Muir, Gregor. "Gillian Wearing." *World Art Magazine* (November), p. 117.

Savage, Jon. "Vital Signs." *Artforum* 32, no. 7 (March), pp. 60–63.

Searle, Adrian. "Gillian Wearing." *Frieze*, no. 18 (September/October), pp. 61–62.

———. "Vox Pop." *Time Out* (January 5–12), p. 42.

1995 Barratt, David. "Gillian Wearing: Hayward Gallery." *Art Monthly*, no. 191 (November), pp. 28–30.

Bonaventura, Paul. "Profile: Wearing Well." *Art Monthly*, no. 184 (March), pp. 24–26.

Buck, Louisa. "British Art: Don't Knock It." *Independent*, June 24, pp. 1, 4.

Cavendish, Dominic. "Gallery Gunslingers on a Shoot to Thrill." *Independent*, September 11, p. 6.

Cork, Richard. "Forthcoming Attractions." *Times Magazine* (November 18).

Corrigan, Susan. "Get the Picture, British Art's Next Superstars." *i-D* (December), pp. 36–49.

Currah, Mark. "Action Replayed." *Time Out* (September 20).

———. "Group Show; Interim Art." *Time Out* (October 11), p. 48.

Feaver, William. "Where There's a Wilt . . ." *Observer*, November 19.

Garnett, Robert. "The British Art Show 4." *Art Monthly*, no. 192 (December/January), pp. 27–28.

Gayford, Martin. "Youth, Formaldehyde, and the Spirit of the Age." *Daily Telegraph Magazine* (November 11).

Hall, James. "Butterfly Ball." *Guardian*, November 14.

———. "Western Security." *Guardian*, September 21.

Harvey, Will. "Bodies of Work." *Observer*, September 9, pp. 10–11.

Januzczak, Waldemar. "Cool Britannia." *Sunday Times*, December 3, Culture section.

Kastner, Jeffrey. "Brilliant." *Art Monthly*, no. 192 (December/January), pp. 10–15.

Kent, Sarah. "Make Believe." *Time Out* (February 22–March), p. 46.

Landesman, Cosmo and Simon Rogers. "Talking Pictures." *The Big Issue*, no. 116 (February 6–12), pp. 12–14.

MacRitchie, Lynn. "Shock Artists." *Financial Times*, November 17.

Morrish, John. "Wildlife, Martyrs to Their Art." *Daily Telegraph Magazine* (October 7), pp. 8–9.

Patrizio, Andrew. "Hayward Shoot Out." *Galleries Guide* (September).

Searle, Adrian. "British Art with Attitude." *Independent*, November 14.

———. "Faces to Watch in the Art World." *Independent*, September 26, p. 8.

———. "These Are the Rising Stars of 1996." *Independent Weekend*, December 30.

Smith, Roberta. "Some British Moderns Seeking to Shock." *New York Times*, December.

Tomkins, Calvin. "London Calling." *New Yorker* (December 11), pp. 115–17.

Walker, Caryn Faure. "Signs of the Times." *Creative Camera* (February/March), pp. 34–37.

CONFESS ALL ON
VIDEO. DON'T WORRY,
YOU WILL BE IN
DISGUISE. INTRIGUED?
CALL GILLIAN.
1994
Color video with sound
30 minutes
Edition of 10 aside from
1 artist's proof

Wearing, Gillian. "Homage to the Woman with the Bandaged Face Who I Saw Yesterday Down Walworth Road." *Blocnotes*, no. 9, pp. 18–19.

———. "A Short Love Story by Gillian Wearing." *Number 3* (September), p. 81.

1996 Bang Larsen, Lars. "Traffic." *Flash Art* 29, no. 189 (summer), pp. 126–27.

Bickers, Patricia. "The Young Devils." *Art Press*, no. 214 (June), pp. 34–35.

Buck, Louisa. "Silver Scene." *Artforum* 34, no. 7 (summer), pp. 34–36.

Garner, Lesley. "Cops on Top in Cauldron." *Daily Express,* August 2, p. 40.

Hall, James. "Letter from London — Towers of London." *Artforum* 34, no. 7 (summer), pp. 31–33.

Judd, Ben. "Interview with Gillian Wearing." *Untitled*, no. 12 (winter 1996/1997), pp. 4–5.

Kent, Sarah. "New Work, Interim Art." *Time Out* (December 11–18), p. 50.

Masterson, Piers. "Imagined Communities." *Art Monthly*, no. 194 (March), pp. 33–35.

Muir, Gregor. "Sign Language." *Dazed and Confused*, no. 25, pp. 52–55.

Shone, Richard. *Made in London.* London: Simmons & Simmons.

Usherwood, Paul. "The Cauldron." *Art Monthly*, no. 198 (July/August), pp. 30–31.

Walters, Guy. "State of the Art." *Times*, July 20.

Wearing, Gillian. "Guest Editor: Gillian Wearing." *Documents sur l'art* (summer), pp. 41–66.

1997 Alberge, Dalya. "All-Women Shortlist Takes Turner by Surprise." *Times*, June 18, p. 5.

———. "Moving Pictures Take Turner Prize." *Times*, December 3, p. 2.

Blazwick, Iwona. "City Nature." *Art Monthly*, no. 207 (June), pp. 7–10.

Buck, Louisa. "Art Project." *Elle Decoration* (December), pp. 84–89.

———. "Life, Art, and the Turner Women." *Evening Standard*, October 28, p. 29.

———. "Three Cheers for Art that Shatters Complacency." *Daily Express*, June 19.

Collings, Matthew. "The New Establishment." *Independent*, August 31, pp. 9–14.

Coomer, Martin. "Gillian Wearing, Chisenhale." *Time Out* (May 21–28).

Dahan, Eric and Gerard Lefort. "Par delà le corps gay et lesbien." *Liberation*, June 28–29.

Decter, Joshua. "Elastic Realities." *Flash Art* (summer), pp. 110–13.

Dorment, Richard. "'Ello, 'ello — What's Going on Here?" *Daily Telegraph,* November 5.

———. "Out of the Mouths of Babes." *Daily Telegraph*, May 21.

Ebner, Jorn. "Tramdeutung und Befragen." *neue bildende kunst* (February/March), p. 80.

Feldman, Melissa E. "Gillian Wearing at Interim Art." *Art in America* 85, no. 7 (July), p. 102.

Fiedler, Peter-Alexander. "Diesen Sommer baden wir in der virtuellen welt." *TLZ Treffpunkt*, no. 672 (July 26).

Fuller, Wendy. "Modern Art? This is Worthy of Constable." *Daily Express*, December 3, p. 4.

BROAD STREET
2001
Six-screen color video
projection with sound
40 minutes
Edition of 2 aside from
2 artist's proofs

Gibbs, Michael. "ID — An International Survey on the Notion of Identity in Contemporary Art." *Art Monthly*, no. 203 (February), pp. 34–36.

Ginn, Kate and Terri Judd. "Constable Picture Wins the Turner (No, Not that Constable)." *Daily Mail*, December 3, p. 17.

Glaister, Dan. "Silence is Golden for Turner Winner." *Guardian*, December 3, p. 5.

———. "A Woman's Place — in the Gallery." *Guardian*, June 18, p. 3.

Goldberg, Vicki. "The Artist Becomes a Storyteller Again." *New York Times*, November 9.

Greene, David A. "Kids." *Village Voice*, October 21, p. 101.

Higgie, Jennifer. "Gillian Wearing." *Frieze*, no. 33 (March/April), p. 80.

Hoge, William. "Arriving in New York after Taking off in London/Video Maker with a Taste for Secrets." *New York Times*, September 14, p. 33.

Jobey, Liz. "A rat race?" *Guardian*, October 4, pp. 28–37.

Johnson, Boris. "Portrait of the Artist of Silent Nuances." *Daily Telegraph*, December 8, p. 34.

Kimmelman, Michael. "Gillian Wearing." *New York Times*, October 24, p. 38.

———. "Gillian Wearing at Jay Gorney." *New York Times*, September 26, p. 37.

Kino, Carol. "True Confessions: Gillian Wearing Puts Britons on the Couch." *Time Out New York* (October 9–16), p. 50.

Laws, Roz. "The Art of Making a £10,000 Video. The 'Failure' from Brum Who Made it to the Top." *Sunday Mercury* (Birmingham), July 13, 1997, p. 13.

Lewis-Smith, Victor. "Kylie at Arm's Length as She Hits Topless C." *Evening Standard*, November 14, p. 31.

Lister, David. "Uproar as Video Entry Snaps up the Turner." *Independent*, December 3, p. 20.

Lyttelton, Celia. "Indecent Exposures." *Esquire* (May), p. 34.

MacMillan, Ian. "Signs of the Times." *Modern Painters* (autumn), pp. 52–55.

Murphy, Fiona. "A Shopping Sensation." *Guardian*, September 27, pp. 56–59.

Reynolds, Nigel. "'Frozen Policemen' Video Wins Turner Prize." *Daily Telegraph*, December 3.

———. "The Turner Shortlist is for Women Only." *Daily Telegraph*, June 18.

Riding, Alan. "No Sexism, Please; They're British." *New York Times*, December 29.

Ronson, Jon. "Ordinarily So: Jon Ronson on Documentary Filmmaking and Gillian Wearing." *Frieze*, no. 36 (September/October), pp. 60–63.

Schierz, Kai Uwe. "Verführung der Kirschtorte." *Thüringen*, no. 30 (July 26).

Searle, Adrian. "Bring on the Naked Dwarf." *Guardian*, May 6, 1997, p. 14.

Searle, Adrian and Nicholas Serota. "Turner Prize Winner: Gillian Wearing's Arresting Image." *Guardian*, December 3, p. 1.

Sewell, Brian. "Why They Banned the Wrong Video." *Evening Standard*, December 19.

Slyce, John. "The Odds on the Turner Prize." *Flash Art* 30, no. 196 (October), p. 49.

Stringer, Robin. "Women Only and Not a Painting in Sight." *Evening Standard*, June 17, p. 30.

Thorncroft, Anthony. "Artist Brushes Paint Aside to Win Turner Prize." *Independent*, December 3, p. 14.

Wearing, Gillian. *Signs that say what you want them to say and Not signs that say what someone else wants you to say.* London: Maureen Paley Interim Art.

Williams, Gilda. "Gillian Wearing." *Art Monthly*, no. 203 (February), pp. 26–27.

1998 Allen, Vaughn. "Hide and Seek." *The Big Issue in the North*, no. 241 (December 28, 1998–January 3, 1999), p. 29.

Cameron, Dan. "Gillian Wearing." In *Cream: Contemporary Art in Culture.* London: Phaidon. Pp. 428–31.

Campbell-Johnston, Rachel. "Wearing: Her Heart on Her Sleeve." *Times*, January 3–9.

Coleman, Sarah. "Interview with Gillian Wearing." *photo metro* 16, no. 149.

Cork, Richard. "Wearing Her Art on Her Sleeve." *Times*, January 13.

Del Re, Gianmarco. "Confessions: Why Would a Businessman Say 'I'm Desperate?' A–Z of Gillian Wearing." *Flash Art* 31, no. 199 (March/April), pp. 88–90.

DiPietro, Monty. "Artist Asks, 'What's Your Sign?'" *Japan Times*, October 24.

Israel, Nico. "Gillian Wearing." *Artforum* 36, no. 5 (January), p. 100.

Kino, Carol. "Cutting Edge, But Comfy." *Atlantic Monthly* (November).

McGann, Paul. "VW Ad Firm Stole My Ideas, Claims Artist." *Independent*, June 12.

Midgley, Carol. "VW Ad Rips off My Work, Says Artist." *Times*, June 12.

Miles, Anna. "Pictura Brittanica, Te Papa Museum, Tongewara." *Artforum* 36, no. 10 (summer), p. 144.

Neumaier, Otto. "Alles bekennen . . . Gespräch mit Gillian Wearing." *noëma art journal*, no. 49 (October/November).

Princenthal, Nancy. "Gillian Wearing." *Art in America* 86, no. 1 (January), pp. 95–96.

Sanger, Daniel. "Declaration of Independents: Seven People Who Choose to Be Different." *Shift* (December/January), p. 42.

Slyce, John. "Wearing a Mask." *Flash Art* 31, no. 199 (March/April), p. 91.

Smith, Roberta. "Art of the Moment, Here to Stay." *New York Times*, February 15, pp. 1, 3.

Stern, Edward. "Translating the Big Idea into Japanese." *Asashi Evening News*, October.

Turner, Grady T. "Gillian Wearing." *BOMB*, no. 63 (spring), p. 34.

"Turner Prize Winner Issues Legal Threat to BMP over VW Ads." *Campaign*, June 12.

"VW Bugs Wearing." *Art Newspaper* (July/August), p. 43.

Williams, Gilda. "Wah-Wah: The Sound of Crying or the Sound of an Electric Guitar." *Parkett*, no. 52, pp. 146–54.

1999 Bennett, Oliver. "Exhibitionist." *Independent Magazine* (May 1), pp. 10–14.

"The British Unveil Another World." *Russia Journal*, December 6–12.

Collings, Matthew. "Rabble Rousing." *Vogue* (October).

Cumming, Laura. "Gillian Wearing, Interim Art." *Observer* (November 7), Art Section p. 10.

Foulkes, Nick. "Her London." *Evening Standard Magazine* (July 23), p. 9.

Gallez, Florence. "Nukes, Lovers Get Their 15 Minutes." *Moscow Times*, November 19.

Gillian Wearing. London: Phaidon.

Gladstone, Neil. "Book Marks: Gillian Wearing." *Nylon* (premiere issue), p. 147.

Grant, Simon. "All about Love." *Guardian Guide*, October 16–22, p. 33.

———. "Why Gillian Is Priceless." *Evening Standard*, June 1.

Greenberg, Sarah. "Gillian Wearing v. Saatchi, The Artist Claims the Ad Man Stole Her Idea." *Art Newspaper*, no. 91 (April), p. 6.

Jones, Jonathan. "What a Scream." *Guardian Review*, October 23, p. 4.

Müller, Donka. "Rewind to the Future." *Bonner* (November).

"Previews: Rewind to the Future." *Contemporary Visual Arts*, no. 26, p. 79.

Rushton, Steve and John Tozer. "Gillian Wearing." *Camera Austria International*, no. 68.

Takano, Yuko. "'99 What's New?" *Figaro* (Japan), no. 150.

Thrift, Julia. "Gillian Wearing, Interim Art." *Time Out* (November 10–17), p. 53.

Titz, Susanne, and Uta Grosenick and Burkhard Reimschneider, eds. "Gillian Wearing." In *Art at the End of the Millennium*. Cologne: Taschen. Pp. 526–29.

Tone, Lillian. "Gillian Wearing." In *The Museum as Muse: Artists Reflect.* New York: The Museum of Modern Art. P. 196.

Wearing, Gillian. "Polaroid Diary." *Observer Magazine* (May 2), p. 11.

"Wears Well." *i-D*, no. 186 (May).

2000   Basilico, Stefano. "Gillian Wearing, *Drunk* and *A Woman Called Theresa*." *Time Out New York* (May 11–18).

Bishop, Claire. "Being Boring." *Untitled*, no. 21.

———. "The Pleasure in Pain." *Evening Standard*, September 27, p. 57.

———. "Uncomfortable Observations." *Untitled*, no. 23, pp. 12–14.

Brown, Neal. "My Name Is Gillian. I Can Turn Your Sad Life into Art." *Independent*, October 1, Culture section, p. 4.

Celant, Germano. "Mirrored Emotions." *Lespresso*, December 12.

Cork, Richard. "Richard Cork's Choice." *Saturday Times*, Play section, October 7–13.

———. "Unmasking Mystery in the Mundane." *Times*, September 27.

Cumming, Laura. "A Staggering Work …" *Observer Review*, September 17, p. 8.

Feaver, William. "Gillian Wearing." *ARTnews* (December), p. 165.

Gorucheva, Tania. "This Other World of Ours." *Flash Art* 33, no. 210 (January/February), p. 62.

Graham-Dixon, Andrew. "Wearing Masks." *Vogue* (September).

Hensher, Philip. "Wearing so Well." *Daily Mail on Sunday*, September 17, p. 78.

Jones, Jonathan. "Down and Out." *Guardian*, September 16.

Kent, Sarah. "Brains of Britain." *Time Out* (July 12–19), p. 51.

———. "Drunken Exploits." *Time Out* (October 4–11), p. 50.

Levin, Kim. "Village Choice: Gillian Wearing." *Village Voice*, May 16.

Lützow, Gunnar. "Zugriff von allen Seiten." *Berliner Morgenpost*, January 15.

Mercer, Kobena. "Ethnicity and Internationality." *Third Text*, no. 49 (winter), pp. 51–62.

Molon, Dominic. "Framed: Gillian Wearing." *Tate: The Art Magazine* (autumn), pp. 20–21.

Müller, Katrin Bettina. "Die Lust der Maschinen." *taz* (January 26).

Myers, Holly. "Beginnings and Endings." *Los Angeles Times*, December 29.

Pilz, Michael. "Frau Hase und der schreckliche Voyeur." *Die Welt*, January 19.

Riding, Alan. "Another Opening, Another Sensation." *New York Times*, September 25, p. B1.

Sawyer, Miranda. "Daring Wearing." *Observer*, September 3, pp. 10–15.

Schwabsky, Barry. "Gillian Wearing, Gorney Bravin + Lee." *Artforum* 39, no. 1 (September), p. 176.

Shone, Richard. "London, Gillian Wearing." *Burlington Magazine* (November).

Slyce, John and Matthew Collings. "Video Art: A Top Twenty." *Modern Painters* 13, no. 2 (summer), pp. 30–33.

Townsend, Chris. "Gillian Wearing." *Hotshoe International* (March/April), p. 14.

Viveros-Faune, Christian. "Fall down, Get up, No Problem." *New York Press* 13, no 19.

Vogel, Carol. "Inside Art: Beemer Shots." *New York Times*, October 13.

2001 "Bekenntnisse in der Badewanne. Grenzgängerin zwischen Voyeurismus und sozialem Engagement: die Britin Gillian Wearing im Kunstraum." *Abendzeitung*, July 9, p. 15.

Bender, Stephen. "Young British Realist." *Reparges* (April).

Berrebi, Sophie. "Génération Sensation." *Connaissance des Arts*, no. 589 (December), pp. 118–27.

Breerette, Geneviève. "Gillian Wearing et Ann-Sofi Sidén, deux vidéastes en quête de réalité." *Le Monde*, April 5.

Colard, Jean-Max and Nicolas Thély. "Bas les masques." *Les Inrockuptibles*, April 10.

Dattenberger, Simone. "Ein schwingendes Ganzes. Kunstverein: Fotos und Videos von Gillian Wearing." *Münchner Merkur*, June 28, p. 17.

"Der Britpop Diskurs. Engagierte kunst oder platter Sozial-Voyerismus? Eine nachgetragene Diskussion zur jüngeren britischen Kunst am Beispiel Gillian Wearing 'Unspoken' im Kunstverein." *go*, July 19–August 1, pp. 78–79.

Gauville, Hervé. "Wearing en âmes titubantes." *Libération*, March 26.

Grimley, Terry. "Rough and Ready, Rich and Raw." *Birmingham Post*, July 26, p. 14.

Gualdi, Stefano. "Gillian Wearing, Fundacio 'la Caixa,' Madrid." *tema celeste*, no. 85 (May/June), p. 81.

Guarda, Israel. "Gillian Wearing." *Número Magazine* (September/October).

Hafner, Hans-Jürgen. "Gillian Wearing: Unspoken." *Kunstforum International* (August/October), pp. 428–29.

Hickling, Alfred. "Nightmare on Broad Street." *Observer Review*, July 22.

Howarth, Sophie. "Pretty Fascinating Boredom." *Tate: The Art Magazine*, no. 24 (spring), pp. 60–66.

Kinnes, Sally. "Report — Gillian Wearing." *Sunday Times*, Culture section.

Michelon, Olivier. "Du document a l'abstraction." *Journal des arts*, March 30.

Newman, Michael. "The Demotic Art of Gillian Wearing." *Parachute*, no. 102 (April/June), pp. 82–101.

Nuridsany, Michel. "Gillian Wearing: De l'émotion avant toute chose." *Le Figaro*, April 20.

Piekenbrock, Marietta. "Hauptdarsteller. Kunst in Zeiten von Talk Show und Reality TV: Gillian Wearing im Kunstverein München." *Frankfurter Rundschau*, July 20.

Robinson, Denise. "In the Middle with You." *Art Press* (March), pp. 22–27.

Rodney, Lee. "Nostalgia and Nationalism/Two London Surveys." *C International Contemporary Art*, no. 70 (summer), pp. 6–7.

Sachs, Brita. "Still sitzt die Polizei. Gillian Wearing im Münchner Kunstverein." *Frankfurter Allgemeine Zeitung*, July 23.

Searle, Adrian. "Brum and Brummer." *Guardian*, July 24.

Sonna, Birgit. "Kunst macht Kinder. Die Turner-Preisträgerin Gillian Wearing zeigt ihre Foto-und Videoarbeiten im Kunstverein München." *Süddeutsche Zeitung*, July 4, p. 14.

Strange, Raimer. *Women Artists in the Twentieth and Twenty-First Century*. Cologne: Taschen.